ESTATE PLANNING SIMPLIFIED

SAFEGUARD YOUR LEGACY WITH WILLS, TRUSTS, AND INHERITANCE FOR EFFECTIVE ASSET MANAGEMENT

RETIREWISE

Copyright © 2024. All rights reserved.

The content within this book may not be reproduced, duplicated, or transmitted without direct written permission from the author or the publisher.

Under no circumstances will any blame or legal responsibility be held against the publisher, or author, for any damages, reparation, or monetary loss due to the information contained within this book, either directly or indirectly.

Legal Notice:

This book is copyright protected. It is only for personal use. You cannot amend, distribute, sell, use, quote, or paraphrase any part of the content within this book, without the consent of the author or publisher.

Disclaimer Notice:

Please note the information contained within this document is for educational and entertainment purposes only. All effort has been expended to present accurate, up-to-date, reliable, and complete information. No warranties of any kind are declared or implied. Readers acknowledge that the author is not engaged in the rendering of legal, financial, medical, or professional advice. The content within this book has been derived from various sources. Please consult a licensed professional before attempting any techniques outlined in this book.

By reading this document, the reader agrees that under no circumstances is the author responsible for any losses, direct or indirect, that are incurred as a result of the use of the information contained within this document, including, but not limited to, errors, omissions, or inaccuracies.

CONTENTS

Introduction	7
1. ESTATE PLANNING: THE WHAT, WHY, AND HOW	9
Defining Estate Planning	10
The Importance of Estate Planning	12
The Process of Estate Planning	15
2. DECODING THE LEGAL LEXICON OF ESTATE PLANNING	19
Understanding Legal Language	22
The Role of Legal Terms in Your Estate Plan	25
3. THE KEYSTONE OF ESTATE PLANNING: WILLS EXPLAINED	29
What Exactly is a Will?	30
The Role of a Will in Estate Planning	32
How to Create a Will	34
What Happens If You Die Without a Will?	37
4. FORTIFYING YOUR LEGACY WITH TRUSTS	41
The Concept of Trusts	42
Different Types of Trusts	46
Setting Up a Trust	48
Trusts and Tax Implications	51
5. ESTATE STRATEGIES FOR EVERY STAGE OF ADULT LIFE	55
Planning for Single Adults	55
Estate Planning for Married Couples	58
Addressing Needs of Blended Families	61
Estate Planning for Unmarried Partners	63
6. SAFEGUARDING YOUR DIGITAL LEGACY	67
Defining Digital Assets	68
The Importance of Including Digital Assets in Your Estate Plan	70

    How to Inventory Your Digital Assets   72
    Steps to Include Digital Assets in Your Estate Plan   74

7. NAVIGATING THE WATERS OF ESTATE TAXES   81
    Understanding Estate Taxes   81
    How to Minimize Estate Taxes   84
    Estate Planning and Income Taxes   88
    State-Specific Estate Tax Laws   91

8. NAVIGATING THE WATERS OF HEALTHCARE
    DIRECTIVES   95
    The Importance of Having a Healthcare Directive   98
    Understanding Power of Attorney   100
    How to Set Up a Healthcare Directive and Power of
    Attorney   103

9. GUARDIANS OF LEGACY: EXECUTORS AND
    TRUSTEES EXPLAINED   107
    The Role of an Executor or Trustee   108
    Factors to Consider When Choosing Your Executor
    or Trustee   110
    The Pros and Cons of Choosing a Professional
    Executor or Trustee   113
    How to Appoint an Executor or Trustee   116

10. CLEAR HORIZONS: THE ESSENTIALS OF
    COMMUNICATING YOUR ESTATE PLAN   121
    The Importance of Communicating Your Estate Plan   122
    Strategies for Effective Communication   124
    How to Handle Difficult Conversations   126
    Planning a Family Meeting   129

11. KEEPING YOUR ESTATE PLAN CURRENT AND
    RELEVANT   133
    When and Why to Update Your Estate Plan   134
    Common Life Events That Require an Update   137
    Reviewing and Updating Your Will and Trusts   140
    Updating Your Healthcare Directive and Power of
    Attorney   142

12. ADAPTING TO THE DIGITAL FRONTIER IN
ESTATE PLANNING 147
Online Tools for Estate Planning 151
The Role of Digital Advisors and Online Legal
Services 154
Staying Updated with Law Changes in the Digital Age 157

Conclusion 163
References 165

INTRODUCTION

Welcome to a journey that is as inevitable as it is imperative: the journey into estate planning. It is a path paved with decisions that shape the legacy we leave behind, a testament to our lives and the care we have for those we cherish.

Understanding the importance of planning your estate cannot be overstated. It involves ensuring that you respect your wishes, protect your assets, and provide for your loved ones as you intend. It is about peace of mind, knowing that you have taken the steps to safeguard the future, regardless of life's unpredictable nature.

Yet, we recognize that the complexity of estate planning can be daunting. Legal terms can seem labyrinthine, the tax implications are often intricate, and the emotional weight of these considerations is indisputably profound. Unsurprisingly, many feel overwhelmed, perhaps even tempted to postpone this crucial task.

We understand that clarity is the antidote to complexity. Each chapter will break down estate planning into its most fundamental components. We will guide you through the essentials of wills and trusts, explain the nuances of various estate planning instruments, and provide you with practical steps to take control of your financial future.

This book offers information and a series of stepping stones to help you build a bridge to your legacy. The following pages aim to serve as your companion, offering the knowledge you need and encouraging you to apply it.

So, let us step forward together. Through real-life scenarios, specific recommendations, and actionable advice, this book will equip you with the tools you need to navigate the process confidently. Your legacy deserves nothing less.

1

ESTATE PLANNING: THE WHAT, WHY, AND HOW

In the tapestry of life, the threads of financial planning and personal wishes intertwine to form the fabric of one's estate. This tapestry, rich with the hues of assets, memories, and desires, is one we weave throughout our lifetime. The act of estate planning, often perceived as a task reserved for the wealthy or the elderly, is, in truth, a practical step that holds significance for every adult. Individuals can ensure that their personal and financial matters are handled according to their wishes upon their passing or incapacitation.

An estate is not solely the sum of one's financial assets; it is an all-encompassing term that includes your possessions, real estate, investments, insurance policies, and digital footprint. To some, it may encompass a collection of fine art; to others, it could mean a cherished family home, or it might simply be a heartfelt letter written to a loved one.

Estate planning is the process of arranging for the management and distribution of a person's estate during and after their life. It encompasses a range of tasks, from drafting a will, setting up trusts, appointing beneficiaries, and making healthcare directives. These steps aim to ensure that an individual's health, wealth, and personal wishes are honored while easing the legal and financial burdens on the bereaved family.

DEFINING ESTATE PLANNING

"Estate" refers to everything you own or control that can be passed on to your heirs or beneficiaries. It is not exclusive to cash, property, and personal belongings but also includes your investments, life insurance proceeds, and even your debts and liabilities. An estate reflects the narrative of your life and the financial footprint you leave behind.

Estate planning is the blueprint for your story once you're no longer here to tell it yourself. It directs who will inherit your assets and how your affairs should be managed. At its core, it represents your voice in decisions that impact the financial well-being and emotional stability of those you care about. This planning involves legal structures and financial tools but is driven by your values, priorities, and the relationships you cherish.

The role of estate planning stretches far beyond deciding who gets what. It is a critical process that can significantly impact the financial security and emotional comfort of your loved ones. It can shield them from the complexities of probate, the legal process where a court oversees the distribution of your estate. With a well-structured plan, you can minimize the taxes levied on your estate, ensuring that your beneficiaries receive more of your assets. Moreover, it can prevent disputes among family members, which often arise during the stressful time following a loss.

The scope of estate planning is broad and dynamic. It is not a one-time event but an ongoing process that evolves with you. Your estate plan should adapt to life's milestones—marriage, the birth of children, significant financial changes, and even shifts in your values and priorities. This plan should be revisited and refined in response to the changing legal landscape and your unique circumstances.

For instance, consider the implications of the digital age on estate planning. In an era where our lives are increasingly online, digital assets such as social media accounts, online banking, and cryptocurrency holdings have become significant components of our estates. These digital assets require the same planning and care as physical assets, ensuring access and control are passed on according to your wishes.

Estate planning also includes making decisions about your healthcare should you become unable to communicate your wishes. Through documents like a living will or a healthcare power of attorney, you can provide instructions on the medical treatment you desire or appoint someone to make decisions on your behalf. This aspect of planning alleviates the burden on family members to make difficult healthcare choices during times of emotional distress.

In reality, estate planning is a form of care—a way to show concern for your own well-being and the welfare of those you may leave behind. It is a tangible expression of love, a method to alleviate potential burdens, and a strategy to preserve your legacy. To illustrate, reflect on a family business that has been the livelihood of multiple generations. Without a comprehensive estate plan, the sudden loss of the owner could plunge the business into uncertainty, affecting not only the immediate family but also employees and customers. By implementing a succession plan and clear directives for the continued operation or sale of the business, the owner can secure the company's future and the financial stability of those dependent on it.

Considering the multifaceted nature of estate planning, it becomes evident that this practice is not an esoteric ritual meant only for those with vast wealth. It is a crucial step for anyone who wishes to take responsibility for their financial and personal legacy. Through planning, you can ensure that your estate—a reflection of your life's work and personal values—is preserved and passed on as you see fit.

THE IMPORTANCE OF ESTATE PLANNING

Estate planning is fundamental to the financial and emotional well-being of those we care about. It's the process of arranging the management of your estate, and it impacts everyone—regardless of the size of the estate or the age of the individual. Let's discuss the significance of estate planning and the inherent benefits it brings.

Ensuring Financial Security

Financial security is a significant concern for many, and rightly so. Estate planning plays a pivotal role in safeguarding the financial future of your heirs. The process involves designating beneficiaries for your assets, which can range from savings accounts to retirement funds; by clearly outlining who receives what and when you minimize the risk of assets being tied up in lengthy court procedures. Moreover, properly designating beneficiaries on life insurance policies and retirement accounts ensures the direct transfer of these funds, bypassing the time-consuming and costly probate process.

Reducing Legal Complications

The absence of an estate plan often leads to legal entanglements that can drag on for years, draining resources and causing unnecessary stress for your loved ones. A well-crafted estate plan includes a valid will, trusts when appropriate, and other legal documents clearly stating your intentions. This plan reduces ambiguity and the likelihood of legal challenges. For instance, a trust can manage your assets effectively, providing a legal structure that outlines how to handle and distribute your assets, with the trustee ensuring the execution of your wishes.

Preserving Family Harmony

Disagreements among family members over inheritance can be emotionally charged and potentially cause long-lasting rifts. Estate planning addresses this by communicating your wishes clearly, thereby reducing the chances of misunderstandings and conflicts. Such planning is about distributing assets, your values, and the relationships you want to nurture even after you're gone. For example, using a personal property memorandum can be effective; it's a document that accompanies your will, allowing you to specify which personal items go to which beneficiaries, thereby preventing potential disputes over sentimental items.

Minimizing Tax Burden

Taxes can take a significant bite out of an inheritance. Strategic estate planning can minimize the tax impact on your estate and your beneficiaries. Techniques such as gifting during your lifetime, establishing specific types of trusts, and taking advantage of tax exemptions can preserve more of your estate for your heirs. It's crucial to stay informed on the ever-evolving tax laws to maximize the benefits of these strategies. The federal estate tax exemption is adjusted for inflation, and it's essential to understand how this impacts asset distribution.

Leaving a Legacy

Estate planning involves considering your legacy and the impact you leave behind. It provides an opportunity to support the causes and organizations that are important to you through bequests. Planning could mean setting up educational funds for grandchildren, donating to a cherished charity, or ensuring the continuation of a family business. A legacy is not solely defined by the financial assets left behind but also by the values and traditions passed on.

A comprehensive estate plan can include an ethical will, a non-binding document allowing you to share your values, experiences, and life lessons with your family. Unlike a traditional will, which focuses on the distribution of assets, an ethical will is about the intangible aspects of your legacy. It's a way to articulate the values you wish to impart, the family traditions you hope will continue, and the personal and moral guidance you want to provide.

In essence, the estate planning process is a clear statement of your financial and personal intentions. It is a testament to your concern for the well-being of those you leave behind, ensuring that your final wishes are respected and that your legacy endures as you envision. It's about putting the pieces in place today so that your story unfolds as you wish tomorrow, providing a sense of continuity and stability in the lives of your loved ones.

THE PROCESS OF ESTATE PLANNING

Embarking on estate planning is akin to preparing for a significant voyage. You wouldn't set sail without a map or a clear destination, and similarly, you should not navigate your financial future without a well-thought-out plan. This process involves several key steps, each building upon the last, to ensure your estate is managed and distributed according to your wishes.

Initial Assessment of Assets

The first step in estate planning is to take stock of what you own. The assessment forms the basis of your plan. It involves listing all your assets, including but not limited to your home, other real estate, bank accounts, investment accounts, retirement funds, life insurance policies, and personal property of value, such as jewelry, art, or collectibles. In addition, you must consider your digital assets, such as social media accounts, online storage, and cryptocurrency holdings.

Equally important is understanding your liabilities—mortgages, loans, credit card debts, and other obligations. An accurate and comprehensive inventory is a snapshot of your financial situation, highlighting the assets that will form part of your estate and those that may require settlement with your estate's assets.

This detailed inventory is not a one-time task. Still, it should be updated regularly to reflect changes such as acquisitions or disposals of assets, fluctuations in value, or changes in your financial situation. Such diligence ensures that your estate plan remains relevant and aligned with your current circumstances.

Setting Estate Objectives

Once your assets and liabilities are clear, the next step is to consider your goals. What do you wish to achieve with your estate? Your objectives might include:

- Ensuring the financial security of a surviving spouse.
- Providing for children's education.
- Supporting a charitable cause.
- Passing on a family business.

Your goals will likely reflect the unique dynamics of your family and life circumstances.

In this stage, it is vital to prioritize your objectives. Sometimes, the goals may conflict, such as wanting to leave a substantial gift to charity while also providing for your family's financial needs. Prioritizing helps in making decisions that align with your most important objectives.

Your objectives will guide the tools and strategies you employ in your estate plan. For instance, if minimizing taxes is a primary goal, specific types of trusts might be appropriate. A special needs trust could be the right tool to ensure a special needs child is cared for. Clearly defining your objectives allows for tailored solutions most effective for your unique situation.

Drafting Essential Documents

Armed with a comprehensive understanding of your assets and a clear set of objectives, you now create the essential documents that will form the backbone of your estate plan. These documents typically include a will, various types of trusts, a power of attorney, and healthcare directives, if applicable.

A will is the fundamental document most people consider when estate planning comes up. It states your wishes regarding the distribution of your assets and can nominate guardians for any minor children. State law dictates asset distribution without a will, which may not align with your preferences.

Trusts are versatile tools that can help achieve various estate objectives, from avoiding probate to reducing estate taxes. There are many kinds of trusts, each serving different purposes. A living trust can manage assets during your lifetime and distribute them after your death without probate.

A power of attorney is a legal document granting someone you trust authority to handle your financial affairs if you become incapacitated. This document can be as broad or as narrow as you wish, granting total control or limiting to specific actions.

Healthcare directives such as a living will, and healthcare power of attorney ensure that your medical preferences are honored if you are unable to communicate them. A living will outlines the types of medical treatment you do or do not want, while a healthcare power of attorney appoints someone to make medical decisions on your behalf.

It is crucial to draft these documents with legal expertise, precision, and clarity to comply with state laws, which vary significantly, and express your wishes unequivocally.

Regular Review and Update

Finally, the fluidity of life necessitates regular reviews and updates to your estate plan. Changes such as marriage, divorce, birth, death, and significant financial shifts can all impact your plan. Additionally, changes in laws may affect various components of your estate plan, especially those related to taxes and asset distribution.

A regular review, ideally annually or after any major life event, ensures that your estate plan remains current and effective. During these reviews, revisit your asset inventory to account for any changes. Reflect on your objectives to ensure they still align with your current wishes. Evaluate the individuals you've designated in roles such as executor, trustee, or healthcare proxy, and consider if these choices still reflect your best interests.

It's crucial to consult with estate planning professionals during this review process. Their expertise helps identify any legal or financial shifts that necessitate adjustments to your plan. They can also guide new strategies or tools that may benefit your estate.

By diligently following these steps—assessing your assets, setting clear objectives, drafting essential documents, and conducting regular reviews—you create a robust estate plan that serves as a blueprint for your legacy. This plan reflects your financial assets and embodies your values and wishes, ensuring they are honored and respected.

2

DECODING THE LEGAL LEXICON OF ESTATE PLANNING

Picture a foreign city with its bustling streets, vibrant markets, and intricate architecture—a place rich in culture and history but where the local tongue is unfamiliar to you. Navigating this city without understanding its language can be both challenging and intimidating. Similarly, the realm of estate planning is replete with its own language, a specialized lexicon that can seem just as foreign and daunting to many. But fear not; with the right guide, you can become fluent in this critical vernacular, transforming what once seemed like legal gibberish into clear, actionable information.

To traverse the landscape of estate planning effectively, one must first become acquainted with the key terms that serve as signposts along the way. These terms are the building blocks of your estate plan—the nouns that name your players and the verbs that drive your actions. Let's introduce and demystify these pivotal terms, giving you the clarity needed to make informed decisions about your estate.

Beneficiary

The beneficiary is the individual or entity you designate to receive the fruits of your labor—the assets and property from your estate. It's like handing over the keys to a treasure chest; the beneficiary is the person you've chosen to open it and benefit from what's inside. Your beneficiaries can include family members, friends, charities, or institutions, and you can specify what you want each to receive, be it a sum of money, a piece of real estate, or a treasured family heirloom.

Executor

The executor is the conductor of your estate's symphony—the person you entrust to orchestrate the fulfillment of your final wishes, as outlined in your will. They are responsible for handling the affairs of your estate, paying off any outstanding debts or taxes, and guaranteeing that your assets are distributed according to your wishes. Choosing the right executor is crucial; this person should be responsible, organized, and willing to commit time to the task. They'll be the ones standing at the helm, guiding your estate through the probate process, acting as the steward of your legacy.

Trustee

A trustee is akin to a guardian of your assets held in trust—a role of honor and obligation. When you set up a trust, you're placing your assets under the trustee's care, who manages and protects these assets for the benefit of the trust's beneficiaries. The trustee wears many hats: an investor, a custodian, and often, a mediator. They must act with the utmost integrity and in the best interest of the beneficiaries, adhering to the trust's terms and navigating the complexities of trust administration.

Power of Attorney

Imagine having a stand-in, someone to step into your shoes and make decisions on your behalf should the need arise. That's the essence of a power of attorney—a legal document that grants another person the authority to act for you, usually in financial or medical matters. This proxy can be granted broad powers, such as handling all your financial affairs, or limited powers, such as selling a specific property. Durable powers of attorney remain in effect even if you become incapacitated, ensuring that someone you trust makes decisions aligned with your preferences.

Probate

Probate is the official proving ground for your will—a court-supervised process that validates your will and oversees the distribution of your estate. Consider it as a safeguard that guarantees payment of your debts and allocation of your assets as per your documented wishes. Probate can be lengthy and public, often involving paperwork, court appearances, and potential legal fees. Many opt for estate planning tools like trusts, which can bypass this process, allowing for a more private and expedited transfer of assets.

Visual Element: Infographic
Understanding Key Estate Planning Terms

A visual diagram that illustrates the relationships and roles of each key term in estate planning:

- **Beneficiary:** Receives assets from the estate or trust.
- **Executor:** Manages and settles the will's directives through probate.

- **Trustee:** Oversees and administers trust assets for beneficiaries.
- **Power of Attorney:** Acts on your behalf in financial or medical decisions.
- **Probate:** Legal process validating the will and overseeing asset distribution.

With these terms clarified, envision how they fit into the broader picture of your estate plan. Each plays a pivotal role in ensuring your intentions are honored, and your estate is cared for. As you continue to build your understanding, remember that the ultimate goal of familiarizing yourself with this language is to create a document and craft a plan that reflects your wishes and provides for those you care about most.

UNDERSTANDING LEGAL LANGUAGE

The lexicon of estate planning can sometimes feel like a dense thicket of terms and phrases, each with nuanced definition and significance. The precision of this language carves a clear path for your intentions, ensuring they are understood and executed as you desire. Unraveling the complexity of this terminology is akin to translating a legal code that governs the passage of your life's accumulations to the next generation.

Decoding Legal Terminology

In this intricate network of estate planning, specific phrases act as keystones, holding the structure of your plan together. Terms such as "intestate" or "testate" determine how your assets are handled with or without a valid will. Understanding these conditions and their consequences allows you to exert control over the distribution process. When transferring ownership, distinguishing between tangible and intangible assets may impact their management and taxation. When transferring ownership, distinguishing between tangible and intangible assets may affect their management and taxation. Tangible assets are physical objects like real estate and artwork, while intangible assets encompass non-physical rights and interests such as stocks or patents.

To navigate effectively, it's crucial to fully understand terms like "codicil." A codicil is an amendment to a will that can modify, add, or revoke sections of the document without requiring a complete rewrite. It is a tool used in estate planning that allows for adjustments to be made without disrupting the overall structure of the will. Another critical term is "per stirpes," a method of distributing an estate that ensures descendants of a beneficiary receive their ancestor's share should the beneficiary pass before the testator. This concept speaks to the distribution of assets and reflects a commitment to family continuity.

Importance of Clear Language

Using clear and concise language is crucial when drafting estate planning documents. This clarity acts as a safeguard, protecting your plan from misinterpretation or disputes. It's the beacon that guides executors and trustees through the fog of complex directives, illuminating the way forward. When drafting these documents, simplicity, and precision are paramount. For example, "fiduciary" should be clearly defined to establish the standard of care expected from the executor or trustee. This person has a fiduciary duty, a legal obligation to act in the best interest of the beneficiaries, with a level of care that is prudent and diligent.

The specificity of language extends to the designation of heirs. It is essential to name each heir individually in your will to prevent confusion and ensure that your assets are distributed as per your wishes. Similarly, in the context of a trust, the language should unambiguously state the "trust corpus," which refers to the assets placed within the trust, and the "trust instrument," which is the document that outlines the trust's terms.

Commonly Misunderstood Terms

Certain terms frequently trip up even the savviest individuals within the fabric of estate planning. When misunderstood, these terms can potentially unravel the intentions behind an estate plan. "Joint tenancy with the right of survivorship" is one such term. It refers to a form of co-ownership where, upon the death of one owner, their interest automatically passes to the surviving co-owner(s). It's a straightforward concept, yet with proper understanding, individuals may realize that this form of ownership supersedes the directives in a will, leading to unintended consequences for asset distribution.

Another commonly misunderstood term is "durable power of attorney," which remains in effect even if the grantor becomes incapacitated. It's often confused with a "general power of attorney," which becomes null and void under the same circumstances. The durability clause is critical; it ensures that the chosen individual can continue managing your affairs when you cannot.

The term "grantor" holds great importance in the world of trusts. The grantor is the person who creates the trust and transfers assets into it. Understanding the grantor's responsibilities and how they affect the trust's management and taxation is crucial. Similarly, the concept of "funded" versus "unfunded" trusts is pivotal. A funded trust has assets placed into it during the grantor's lifetime, whereas an unfunded trust consists only of the trust agreement with no assets transferred until later, often at the grantor's death.

In the dance of estate planning, even seemingly simple terms like "gift" carry layers of meaning. In legal parlance, a gift is a transfer of property for which no consideration is expected or received in return. The act of gifting can serve as a strategic tool for estate planning, allowing the transfer of wealth during one's lifetime and potentially reducing the taxable estate. Proper documentation and adherence to annual gifting limits are essential to avoid tax liabilities when gifting.

This level of comprehension gives you the power to craft an estate plan that serves as a testament to your life and values. With a firm grasp of the legal language, you can ensure that every clause and codicil of your plan serves its intended purpose, honoring your wishes and providing for your loved ones with the utmost fidelity. As we continue to explore the nuances of estate planning, remember that each term you encounter is more than just a word—it's a vessel carrying the weight of your intentions. This beacon lights the path for your legacy to follow.

THE ROLE OF LEGAL TERMS IN YOUR ESTATE PLAN

Navigating the intricate fabric of estate planning necessitates a keen understanding of legal terminology, as the specific words used in your documents can significantly impact their effectiveness and enforceability. Let us explore the critical legal terms that serve as pillars in the architecture of wills, trusts, and powers of attorney. These terms act as the DNA of your estate plan, each sequence encoding vital instructions that will shape its execution.

Legal Terms in Wills

A will is akin to a map that guides your loved ones through the distribution of your estate, and the language employed within it must be precise and unequivocal. One such term is "testator," who creates the will. It is your role as the testator to designate "heirs," who are the individuals entitled to your assets by law, and "legatees," who are specifically named to receive particular property or amounts.

The residue of an estate is what's left after debts, taxes, and specific bequests are paid. It is often left to a residuary beneficiary, typically a close family member or a spouse, who will receive the balance of your assets. To avoid any potential confusion, it is vital to clearly identify this party and any alternates in case your primary choice predeceases you.

A will may also contain a "no-contest clause" intended to deter beneficiaries from challenging your will. Such a clause, however, must be drafted with care, as its enforceability varies from state to state.

Furthermore, including a "simultaneous death clause" guides asset distribution should you and a beneficiary die concurrently or within a short period of one another. This term ensures that your estate plan contemplates even the most unforeseen events, thereby preventing your assets from becoming subject to default state laws that may not reflect your intentions.

Legal Terms in Trusts

In trusts, the terminology shapes the vessel that holds and protects your assets for the benefit of your chosen recipients. A "settlor" or "grantor" is the person who establishes the trust, transferring assets into it. The "trust property" or "principal" refers to the assets that fund the trust. At the same time, "income" describes the earnings generated from these assets, which may be distributed to beneficiaries according to the terms you set forth.

The "trust instrument" is the trust's governing document, and within it, terms like "irrevocable" and "revocable" determine the degree of control retained over the trust. An irrevocable trust generally cannot be altered once established, while a revocable trust permits modifications during the settlor's lifetime.

A "spendthrift clause" protects a beneficiary from creditors by prohibiting the beneficiary's interest from being assigned or reached by creditors before the trust distributes the assets. It is a safeguard for the assets within the trust, ensuring that they are used as intended for the benefit of the beneficiary rather than to pay off the beneficiary's debts.

When distributing trust assets, terms like "discretionary distributions" grant the trustee the power to decide when and how much to allocate to beneficiaries, often based on a standard, such as health, education, maintenance, and support. This flexibility allows the trustee to manage the trust assets in response to the beneficiaries' changing needs and circumstances.

Legal Terms in Power of Attorney

A power of attorney is a robust tool in estate planning, allowing you to appoint an "agent" or "attorney-in-fact" to act on your behalf in financial or healthcare matters. The "principal" in this context refers to the person granting the power, which is you.

The "capacity" of the principal is a critical term, as it relates to the individual's ability to understand and make decisions. The power of attorney document must specify the circumstances under which it becomes effective or ceases to be in effect, especially in the case of a "springing power of attorney," which only becomes active upon the occurrence of a specific event, typically the principal's incapacitation.

The "scope" of authority granted to the agent can be as broad or as narrow as the principal desires, delineated by terms such as "general," giving wide-ranging powers, or "limited," confining the agent's authority to specific matters.

Understanding these terms and their nuances is vital to creating a power of attorney that accurately conveys your intentions and gives your agent appropriate control. It is an instrument of delegation that, when crafted with precision, can provide peace of mind and continuity in managing your affairs should you be unable to do so yourself.

The words we choose in our estate planning documents are more than mere placeholders; they are the messengers of our deepest wishes and directives. They carry the weight of our intentions and the power to enact them. As you reflect upon the legal terms that will form the cornerstone of your estate plan, consider them your allies—tools that, when wielded with understanding and precision, build a fortress around your legacy, ensuring that it stands firm against the tides of time and change.

As you turn these pages, you continue to fortify your knowledge, layering brick upon brick until the structure of your estate plan stands complete and resolute. It is a plan that, in its final form, will not only speak with your voice but will do so with the clarity and authority that your legacy deserves.

3

THE KEYSTONE OF ESTATE PLANNING: WILLS EXPLAINED

Imagine you're about to paint a picture that illustrates your life's achievements, values, and care for loved ones. Instead of relying on brushes and colors, you possess something far more powerful and enduring: your will. This document, often perceived as the cornerstone of estate planning, is not a mere formality but an expression of your life's narrative, ensuring that your story doesn't end with your last breath but continues as you envisioned.

A will is your voice in a future where you won't be present to speak. It's a declaration of your intentions, a protective shell around your assets, and a guide for those you leave behind. With it, you chart a course for the future, one that honors your wishes and upholds your legacy.

WHAT EXACTLY IS A WILL?

Purpose of a Will

The primary purpose of a will is to communicate your wishes regarding the distribution of your assets after your passing. Think of it as the director of an orchestra, guiding each instrument to play its part at the right time, ensuring the harmony of the final piece. A will can be as straightforward as bequeathing everything to a single person or as intricate as assigning specific items to various individuals and organizations. It's not just about who gets what; it's also about who will manage the process, care for your minor children, and look after your pets.

Basic Structure of a Will

The will is a legal document that provides clarity and direction by identifying the person it belongs to, known as the testator. It typically follows a specific order of instructions, starting with a declaration of intent, followed by revoking previous wills, and ending with the appointment of an executor responsible for carrying out the instructions. The main body of the will outlines the distribution of assets, including bank accounts and family heirlooms, and may also include the appointment of guardians for minor children. Finally, the will concludes with the testator's and witnesses' signatures, signifying validity.

Imagine you're crafting a recipe that your family will follow to recreate your favorite dish. Your will, like that recipe, details the essential ingredients (your assets), the method (instructions for distribution), and the preferred outcome (your intended beneficiaries enjoying the meal). It's a blend of precision and personal touch that results in a lasting legacy.

Legal Requirements for a Valid Will

For a will to hold up as a binding legal document, it must meet specific criteria. These vary by jurisdiction but commonly include the testator being of legal age and sound mind, meaning they understand the nature of the will and its consequences. The will should be written willingly, without any external pressure or influence from others. It usually requires the testator's signature and those of witnesses who attest to the testa or's capacity and free will in signing the document. Some states allow for "holographic" wills handwritten by the testator; in some cases, these may not even require witnesses.

Consider the act of securing your signature on an important contract. It's a moment that signifies agreement, intent, and commitment. Similarly, signing a will is a pivotal event that cements your decisions and sets them into motion.

Visual Element: Checklist
Essentials of a Valid Will

- Testator's full name and statement of intent
- Revocation of previous wills or codicils
- Appointment of an executor
- Detailed asset distribution
- Guardianship designations (if applicable)
- Testator's signature
- Witnesses' signatures
- Notarization (depending on state requirements)

A will's power lies in its details— the specificity with which it outlines who gets what. For example, leaving a family business to a child who has shown interest and aptitude can ensure the enterprise's continuing success, reflecting your pride in the legacy you've built. Or, assigning a cherished piece of jewelry to a dear friend can serve as a tangible reminder of a bond that transcends time.

Understanding the purpose and structure of a will and the legal requirements for its validity forms the bedrock of effective estate planning. In the following sections, we'll explore how to create a will that faithfully reflects your intentions and safeguards your legacy, ensuring that your final wishes are honored and your loved ones are cared for according to your plan.

THE ROLE OF A WILL IN ESTATE PLANNING

A will serves as the blueprint for orchestrating one's estate after one's departure, providing explicit directions to ease the transfer of assets, the care of minors, and the responsibilities bestowed upon the chosen executor. This document ensures that personal wishes are executed precisely for estate planning.

Distribution of Assets

The allocation of one's assets is a personal affair reflective of relationships, affections, and the legacy one wishes to leave. A will delineate who inherits property, monetary ass ts, family heirlooms, and other personal belongings. In this document, you may detail the division of assets with granularity, assigning particular items or specific monetary amounts to individuals or organizations. This assignment can include leaving particular pieces of real estate to heirs or bequeathing donations to favored charities.

Without a will, the state assumes control over the distribution process, applying a one-size-fits-all approach to a situation that often requires a tailored fit. This formulaic division of assets ignores personal connections and stories, potentially conflicting with the deceased's desires and beneficiaries' needs. A will, therefore, is essential to ensure that each asset is passed on according to the owner's express instructions, reflecting their decisions and values.

Appointment of Guardians for Minors

For parents and guardians, the well-being of their minor children is paramount. In the unfortunate event of the parent's untimely demise, a will becomes the vehicle for expressing their wishes regarding the children's future care. Within its clauses, parents can appoint a guardian they trust to raise their children with the same values and care they would provide.

Determining guardianship within a will is a thoughtful process, often involving heartfelt discussions with potential guardians to ensure they are willing and able to take on such a responsibility. This consideration also extends to the financial arrangements made for the children's upbringing, which can be addressed by establishing trusts within the will. By making these decisions, parents offer their children stability and continuity of care, even in their absence.

Naming an Executor

An executor is the individual entrusted with the duty of enacting the provisions of the will. This role extends beyond merely distributing assets; it encompasses managing the estate's affairs, settling debts and taxes, and, often, making pivotal decisions during the probate process. Selecting an executor is a decision imbued with trust and foresight, as this person will be at the helm, steering the estate through the intricacies of fulfillment.

When naming an executor, consider the individual's capability, integrity, and willingness to commit time and energy to the task ahead. The executor must navigate the legal landscape, coordinate with beneficiaries, and sometimes resolve conflicts that arise. Selecting someone equipped with both the insight for the administrative aspects and the empathy to handle delicate family dynamics is crucial for the smooth execution of the will.

In assigning this role, the testator can provide the executor with guidance and resources through a letter of instruction or by establishing clear lines of communication with the estate's attorney and financial advisor. This foresight eases the executor's burden, allowing them to act confidently and align with the testator's intentions.

Each of these elements—the distribution of assets, the appointment of guardians for minors, and the naming of an executor—plays a vital role in the tapestry of estate planning. Together, they ensure that the testator's wishes are not left to interpretation or chance but executed with the care and precision they deserve. A will, therefore, is not a mere document but a testament to one's life and values, a final act of consideration for those left behind, and a definitive statement of one's legacy.

HOW TO CREATE A WILL

Inventory of Assets

The first step in creating a w ll is compiling a thorough inventory of your assets. This task is akin to assembling the puzzle pieces that, when complete, will reveal the full picture of your estate. List tangible assets such as real estate, vehicles, jewelry, and artwork. Remember items of sentimental value; these often hold immeasurable worth to those you love. Next, detail your financial assets: bank accounts, stocks, bonds, retirement accounts, and life insurance policies. Make sure to securely document usernames and passwords for online accounts for the executor, as digital assets are also a part of your estate. Consider liabilities as well, such as mortgages, loans, and credit card debts, as these will impact the net value of your estate.

Creating a comprehensive list of assets and liabilities provides a clear starting point for distributing your estate and assists your executive in accurately managing and settling your affairs. Please don't rush this step; it ensures you account for everything you own and pass it on according to your wishes.

Decision on Beneficiaries

Selecting your beneficiaries is the next pivotal step after accounting for your assets. Reflect on those who have touched your life and whom you wish to acknowledge or support. Beneficiaries include family, friends, charitable organizations, or educational institutions. When deciding on beneficiaries, consider the impact of your legacy. For some, a financial inheritance can provide educational opportunities or be a foundation for future security. For others, a particular item may hold deep emotional significance, serving as a lasting reminder of your relationship.

In making these decisions, it's essential to be clear and specific to avoid ambiguity and potential conflict. If a particular asset has multiple prospective beneficiaries, contemplate the division carefully. Discussing with these individuals to gauge their feelings and expectations regarding potential inheritances might be prudent. These conversations can also help avoid surprises and ensure your decisions align with the beneficiaries' circumstances and needs.

Drafting the Will

With a comprehensive asset inventory and a clear decision on beneficiaries, you are ready to draft the will. This step is where the elements of your estate plan merge into a formal legal document. Engage the services of an estate planning attorney to ensure that yours will adhere to state laws and truly reflect your intentions. An attorney can also advise on complex situations, such as providing for a special needs beneficiary or structuring your estate to minimize tax implications.

Approach the drafting process with thoroughness and attention to detail. Craft each clause to convey your wishes unambiguously. Consider including alternate beneficiaries in case your primary choices predecease you. If you have minor children, the will should nominate a guardian and establish a trust to manage any inheritance until they reach adulthood. Remember to periodically review your will to ensure it reflects your current situation and desires. Remember, you can continually update it as circumstances change.

Witnessing and Signing the Will

The final step in creating a will is the formal signing and witnessing process, essential for the document's legal validity. Witnesses to a will are typically required to be disinterested parties—meaning they do not stand to benefit from the will. One must maintain impartiality to ensure fairness and prevent potential disputes regarding the will's authenticity.

When you sign the will, do so in the presence of your witnesses, who must also sign the document, attesting to your capacity and voluntary action. The number of witnesses required can vary by jurisdiction, so following your state's specific regulations is critical.

In some cases, the signing may also need to be notarized, adding a layer of certification to the document's authenticity.

Signing the will is more than a formality; it is an affirmation of your decisions and a pivotal moment that sets your estate plan into motion. Once signed and witnessed, your will stands as a legally binding document that articulates your final wishes and provides the blueprint for the distribution of your estate. It is an enduring expression of your life's narrative, crafted to ensure your legacy is honored and your loved ones are supported as you intended.

WHAT HAPPENS IF YOU DIE WITHOUT A WILL?

Without a will, an individual's estate becomes an open narrative, with endings not authored by the deceased but written by state laws. Intestate succession laws govern the distribution of assets when a person dies without leaving behind a will. These laws may result in outcomes that differ significantly from the individual's preference.

State Laws on Intestate Succession

A set of regulations specific to each state dictates the division of assets when there is no will. These laws create a default distribution plan, typically favoring the closest relatives—spouses, children, and parents. Without immediate family, the estate may pass to more distant kin, following a hierarchy that the state deems equitable. The rigidity of these laws does not account for the nuances of personal relationships or individual circumstances. Intestate succession does not recognize a lifelong friend or a charitable cause close to the deceased's heart.

To illustrate, if a single individual with no children passes away, their parents might inherit the estate, even if the individual had a more distant relative or friend they would have preferred to benefit.

Depending on the jurisdiction, married individuals may pass on the entirety of their estate to their surviving spouse or divide it among their spouse, siblings, and parents. These outcomes can vastly differ from what the deceased might have intended, highlighting the importance of drafting a will to fulfill personal wishes.

Potential Disputes Among Heirs

When potential heirs need the guidance of a will, they often engage in disputes over the estate. In the face of unclear directives, emotions can run high, and disagreements may arise regarding the rightful recipients of assets.

When questioning the fairness of state-mandated distributions, disputes can become more intense, especially when sentimental or valuable assets are involved. The potential for conflict extends beyond the immediate aftermath of a person's death, as the effects of a contentious probate process can leave lasting scars on relationships and tarnish the memory of the deceased.

Probate Process Without a Will

The probate process without a will is a public affair where the court oversees the distribution of the estate. This procedure can be time-consuming and costly, diminishing the estate's value through legal fees and court costs. The court appoints an administrator, a role similar to an executor, to manage the estate's affairs. This individual may not have intimate knowledge of the deceased's wishes or relationships, which can lead to decisions that may not align with what the deceased would have wanted.

The administrator's duties include locating legal heirs, managing and liquidating assets, paying debts and taxes, and distributing the remaining assets according to state laws. Without the deceased's input, this process can become a mechanical distribution of assets, void of the personal touch that a well-crafted will provides.

The impersonal statutes will be responsible for distributing the deceased's estate without a will, and the deceased's true intentions may never surface. This underscores the significance of taking the reins of one's estate planning to ensure that the legacy left behind is one of choice, not chance.

Ultimately, the absence of a will can result in a narrative far removed from one's life story, with final chapters that may not reflect the bonds and values held dear. It is a stark reminder of the pivotal role estate planning plays in preserving one's wishes and the harmony of those left to remember and honor a life lived. With careful planning and a clear will, the legacy left behind can be a true testament to the life and love shared rather than a tale of unintended consequences and legal dictates.

The next chapter will build upon this foundation, exploring the intricate weave of trusts. This tool offers control over asset distribution and potential benefits in privacy, tax planning, and managing complex family dynamics. The discussion will illuminate the types of trusts available and their advantages, guiding you to make informed choices that align with your estate planning goals.

4

FORTIFYING YOUR LEGACY WITH TRUSTS

Imagine a treasure chest, ornate and timeless, safeguarding precious jewels and heirlooms. This chest is not hidden away but entrusted to a guardian who ensures your treasures are protected, managed, and ultimately gifted to those you've chosen. In estate planning, this chest is not a figment of pirate lore but a trust—a powerful instrument designed to hold and secure your assets with the same commitment to safeguarding your legacy as you would.

Trusts are not merely tools of the wealthy; they are adaptable instruments that can serve many purposes, from charitable giving to special needs planning, offering benefits that extend beyond the simplistic division of assets. In this chapter, we'll explore what a trust is, the roles of those involved, and the various types of trusts, providing an understanding of how they can be integrated into your estate planning to serve your unique objectives.

THE CONCEPT OF TRUSTS

Definition of a Trust

At its core, a trust is a fiduciary arrangement, a relationship bound by trust and confidence. It allows a third party, or trustee, to hold assets on behalf of a beneficiary or beneficiaries. It's a legal entity you create to take title to your assets, but it's more than just a holding space. You set forth specific guidelines for managing assets in a trust with a commitment and promise to benefit those you choose.

Think of a trust like a legal greenhouse, where you carefully plant your assets, and a chosen gardener—the trustee—tends to them. Like delicate seedlings, these assets can grow and flourish under the trustee's care until it's time to pass them on to your beneficiaries, just as you've directed. This process can occur during your lifetime or after your passing, depending on the type of trust you establish.

Parties Involved in a Trust

Establishing a trust brings together three critical roles: the grantor, the trustee, and the beneficiary. Each has a distinct part to play in this legal relationship.

- The Grantor: Also known as the settlor or trustor, the grantor is the person who creates the trust, sets the terms, and transfers assets into it. You, the artist, paint the future of your assets and decide how and when they will be distributed.
- The Trustee: The individual or institution the grantor appoints to manage the trust's assets. The trustee's role is vital; they must act with prudence and loyalty, putting the

beneficiaries' interests above all else. It's a role that requires a steadfast commitment to the grantor's intentions.
- The Beneficiary: These are the individuals or entities the grantor designates to benefit from the trust. Beneficiaries may receive income from the trust during its term, distribution of assets at a specified time, or other benefits as directed by the grantor.

The trust document governs the roles of each party, as they are integral to the function of the trust. The terms laid out in the document direct this legal ensemble.

Types of Trusts

Trusts come in many shapes and sizes, each with features and benefits. Here's a glimpse into the variety:

- Living Trusts (Inter Vivos): Created during the grantor's lifetime, these trusts can be either revocable or irrevocable. They enable the management of assets while the grantor is alive and stipulate the distribution after death.
- Testamentary Trusts: These are established through a will and come into effect after the grantor's death. They provide a way to manage and protect beneficiaries' assets over time.
- Charitable Trusts: These trusts are designed to benefit a charitable organization or cause and may offer the grantor tax benefits.
- Special Needs Trusts: Tailored trusts for beneficiaries with disabilities ensure they qualify for government assistance programs.
- Spendthrift Trusts: These protect the trust's assets from being claimed by a beneficiary's creditors.

- Marital or "A" Trust: Beneficial for a surviving spouse, this trust often provides income and principal as needed and may offer estate tax benefits.

Visual Element: Chart
A Snapshot of Trust Types and Their Functions

Type of Trust

- **Description**
- **Primary Benefit**

Living Trust (Revocable)

- Created during the grantor's life and can be altered.
- Flexibility and control during the grantor's life.

Living Trust (Irrevocable)

- Cannot be altered once established.
- Asset protection and potential tax benefits.

Testamentary Trust

- Established through a will after death.
- Management of assets for beneficiaries over time.

Charitable Trust

- Established to benefit a charitable organization.
- Charitable giving and tax advantages.

Special Needs Trust

- Provides for a beneficiary with disabilities.
- Ensures government assistance eligibility.

Spendthrift Trust

- Protects assets from beneficiaries' creditors.
- Asset protection for beneficiaries.

Marital Trust

- Provides for a surviving spouse.
- Income for spouse and potential estate tax benefits.

The selection of a trust type is as personal as choosing a home. You must consider the size, structure, and location—all attributes that align with your needs and goals. Just as you would select a cozy cottage for its charm and warmth or a modern loft for its efficiency and style, you choose a trust based on the protection, management, and benefits it offers to your estate.

In the following sections, we will delve further into the distinct types of trusts, providing insights to determine which one or combination best aligns with your estate planning objectives. The choices are varied and valuable, from revocable living trusts that offer flexibility and control to irrevocable trusts that provide asset protection and tax advantages. We'll explore how each trust functions and its unique advantages, empowering you with the knowledge to select the perfect trust to fortify your legacy.

DIFFERENT TYPES OF TRUSTS

Revocable Trusts

A revocable trust is a dynamic estate planning tool, offering the grantor flexibility that other trusts do not. The grantor can alter, amend, or even dissolve this type of trust entirely at their discretion as long as they are alive and mentally competent. The adaptability of a revocable trust makes it an attractive option for those who seek to maintain control over their assets while also planning for the future.

Imagine a revocable trust as a living, breathing document that grows and changes with you through various life stages. It allows you to appoint yourself as the trustee, overseeing the assets and making changes as circumstances evolve—whether that's the birth of a grandchild, the acquisition of new property, or a change in marital status. Upon the grantor's death, the revocable trust typically becomes irrevocable, securing the assets for beneficiaries and often bypassing the public and meticulous probate process.

Irrevocable Trusts

In contrast to their adaptable counterparts, irrevocable trusts are steadfast agreements. Once established, they cannot be modified or rescinded. This permanence offers distinct advantages concerning asset protection and potential tax benefits. By transferring assets into an irrevocable trust, you effectively remove them from your estate, shielding them from future creditors and reducing your taxable estate.

Crafting an irrevocable trust is a gesture of forward-thinking commitment. It requires a level of certainty about the disposition of one's assets that is not necessary with revocable trusts. However, for those looking to mitigate estate taxes, protect wealth from legal judgments, or preserve assets for specific purposes such as special needs planning or philanthropy, an irrevocable trust can be an invaluable component of their estate strategy.

Testamentary Trusts

A testamentary trust, often called a will trust, emerges from the provisions outlined in a will. This trust does not exist until after the grantor's death, at which point it is irrevocable. Testamentary trusts serve many purposes, including providing structured support to beneficiaries who may not be prepared for a lump-sum inheritance or ensuring that a surviving spouse is taken care of before the remaining assets are distributed to other beneficiaries.

The creation of a testamentary trust is a thoughtful process. To form the trust, you must include a clause in your will that specifies the assets to fund it and the beneficiaries who will receive support. Testamentary trusts offer a tiered approach to asset distribution, often used to stagger inheritances over time or until certain conditions are met, such as a beneficiary reaching a specific age or milestone.

Living Trusts

Living trusts, formally inter vivos trusts, are established during the grantor's lifetime. Depending on the grantor's goals and needs, they can be either revocable or irrevocable. Living trusts are a proactive approach to estate planning, allowing you to place assets within the trust while you're still alive, with the option to benefit from them before they pass on to your heirs.

One of the primary advantages of a living trust is its ability to bypass probate. Assets within a living trust can be transferred directly to beneficiaries without court involvement, expediting the distribution process and maintaining privacy. Living trusts also provide an avenue for managing your assets should you become incapacitated, as you can name a successor trustee who will manage the trust's affairs according to your established terms.

Each type of trust serves a specific purpose and offers benefits tailored to different situations. Whether seeking flexibility and control, asset protection, tax efficiency, or planning for incapacity, there's a trust structure that can align with your estate planning objectives. These trusts' careful selection and customization create a fortified legacy, ensuring that your assets are preserved, protected, and passed on according to your most profound intentions.

SETTING UP A TRUST

Establishing a trust is akin to preparing a tailored suit; the fit must be perfect for the intended purpose. The meticulous process involves several steps, each critical to ensuring that the trust operates effectively and aligns with your long-term intentions.

Choosing the Right Type of Trust

The initial stage in setting up a trust is akin to selecting the right material for that suit. It requires thoroughly understanding the various trust fabrics available and their properties. You must assess your circumstances, financial goals, and the needs of your beneficiaries.

For instance, if your priority is to retain the ability to modify the trust, a revocable trust might suit your needs, offering the flexibility to adjust terms or dissolve the trust entirely. On the other hand, if asset protection and estate tax reduction are your primary goals, an irrevocable trust could provide a sturdy framework, insulating your assets from claims and reducing taxable estate size.

The choice becomes more nuanced when considering specialized trusts. Should you wish to set aside funds for a beneficiary with a disability, a special needs trust ensures they receive the care they require without jeopardizing their eligibility for public assistance. Alternatively, if philanthropy is close to your heart, a charitable remainder trust could fulfill your desire to give back while delivering certain tax advantages.

This stage demands careful consideration and, often, the guidance of an estate planning professional who can illuminate the paths each trust type offers and help you select the one that aligns with your unique tapestry of needs and aspirations.

Naming the Trustee

Once the type of trust is selected, attention turns to appointing the trustee, a critical decision that shapes the trust's operation. The trustee's role is multifaceted, encompassing asset management, distribution to beneficiaries, and adherence to the trust's terms. Remember that this individual needs to be trustworthy and competent, as they will manage your assets and carry out your instructions.

In selecting a trustee, evaluate candidates based on their integrity, financial acumen, and ability to navigate complex legal and fiduciary responsibilities. For some, a family member or close friend may embody these qualities, offering a personal connection to the beneficiaries and an intimate understanding of your wishes. Others may opt for a professional trustee, such as a trust attorney or a financial institution, which can bring neutrality, expertise, and experience to the role.

It is also prudent to designate a successor trustee who can step in should the original trustee not fulfill their duties. This ensures the continuation of managing and distributing the trust's assets, thus preserving the integrity of your estate plan.

Transferring Assets into the Trust

With the trustee in place, the process moves to transferring assets into the trust and establishing the trust's funding. This transfer is not merely a transaction but a deliberate placement of your chosen assets under the trust's protection.

The trust must transfer the deed of tangible assets, like real estate, into its name. The account holder must re-title financial accounts and formally assign personal belongings. For certain assets, such as life insurance or retirement accounts, the trust must be named as the beneficiary to ensure that these assets flow into the trust upon your passing.

The transfer is a detailed operation that demands accuracy to prevent oversights that could lead to assets being left outside the trust's purview, potentially subjecting them to probate or disputes. Creating a comprehensive list of assets and methodically working through each, confirming their integration into the trust is advisable.

Securities, for example, may require coordination with financial institutions to ensure proper transfer. Similarly, business interests might necessitate agreements that respect existing ownership structures while aligning with the trust's terms.

It may be beneficial to transfer some assets into the trust incrementally, especially if there are potential tax implications to consider. Engaging with tax advisors or estate planning attorneys can provide clarity and ensure that you execute the transfers in a manner that supports your financial strategy. This step may be complex, but seeking professional advice can help simplify the process.

Each asset transitioned into the trust weaves another thread into the fabric of your estate plan. This careful integration ensures that the trust is fully prepared to safeguard your assets and, when the time comes, to transfer them seamlessly to your beneficiaries.

Establishing a trust is a process that demands thoughtful deliberation, meticulous planning, and strategic execution. It reflects your attention to detail and commitment to effectively providing for your beneficiaries. With the correct type of trust in place, a reliable trustee at the helm, and a thorough transfer of assets, the trust stands ready to fulfill the vital role it plays in your estate plan.

TRUSTS AND TAX IMPLICATIONS

Various tax threads interweave the fabric of estate planning, shaping your financial tapestry's overall design and impact. Trusts, in particular, play a pivotal role in this regard, offering mechanisms that can alter the tax landscape of your estate. Navigating these waters with an informed mind is crucial, recognizing how trusts can interact with different tax obligations and possibly turn the tide in your favor.

Estate Tax Considerations

Estate taxes can significantly affect the value of your beneficiaries' inheritance when they subject the transferred assets upon death. Trusts can serve as strategic vessels, skillfully navigating these tax-infused waters. For example, certain irrevocable trusts can remove assets from your taxable estate, potentially lowering the estate tax liability.

Consider a bypass trust, which can shelter assets up to the estate tax exemption amount upon the first spouse's death. This can create a safe harbor for these assets and prevent them from being swept into the surviving spouse's taxable estate. The benefit is twofold: it preserves the exemption for the first spouse while securing assets for beneficiaries, often the couple's children, independent of the surviving spouse's estate.

Income Tax Considerations

The currents of income tax also flow through the world of trusts, with distinct considerations for the grantor, the trust itself, and the beneficiaries. Trusts can generate income through their assets, and this income is subject to taxation. However, the responsibility for payment can vary.

In the case of revocable trusts, the grantor typically bears the income tax responsibility as they retain control over the assets. Conversely, irrevocable trusts often pay their income taxes, which can be at higher rates than individual taxes. However, if such a trust distributes income to beneficiaries, that income shifts to their tax returns, potentially creating a tax-saving windfall if they are in lower brackets.

Therefore, the strategic use of trusts can influence the flow of income taxes, either directing them to the trust itself or allocating them to beneficiaries to optimize the overall tax impact on the estate.

Gift Tax Considerations

When transferring assets into an irrevocable trust, it's essential to consider gift tax, as it becomes another factor in the trust equation. Many consider these transfers taxable gifts, but you can structure them to utilize annual gift tax exclusions and lifetime exemption amounts.

The careful timing and structuring of asset transfers into a trust can maximize these exemptions. For instance, spreading out transfers over multiple years can leverage the annual gift tax exclusion, reducing the overall gift tax burden. Additionally, by applying a portion of the lifetime gift tax exemption to larger transfers, you can mitigate the gift tax impact while funding the trust.

Generation-Skipping Transfer Tax Considerations

The generation-skipping transfer (GST) tax is a tax on assets transferred to individuals two or more generations below the grantor, such as grandchildren. Using trusts can help navigate these GST tax waters with agility.

Specifically designed trusts, like the dynasty trust, can provide for multiple generations while minimizing the impact of GST taxes. By allocating the GST tax exemption to transfers into the trust, the grantor can protect assets as they cascade down through the family lineage, often bypassing GST taxes for generations.

With each twist and turn in the tax landscape, trusts offer options to shield your assets and ensure your beneficiaries receive the full benefit of your legacy. Understanding these tax implications is essential in charting a course that minimizes tax liabilities and aligns with your vision for your estate.

Navigating the intricate tax implications of trusts resembles a captain steering a ship through a maze of channels and currents. Each decision can significantly alter the course, dictating the final destination of your assets and the legacy they represent. It requires vigilance, knowledge, and the foresight to anticipate how each move can affect the future of your estate.

In trust planning, the tax element is a dynamic force that shapes the structure and effectiveness of the trust. It is an area where expert guidance can be invaluable, providing the clarity to make informed decisions and the strategies to optimize your estate for tax purposes. This knowledge makes designing a trust that guides your assets safely to your chosen beneficiaries more accessible.

As we continue to weave the narrative of estate planning, it becomes clear that trusts are more than mere vessels for asset management—they are powerful instruments that can shape your estate's tax narrative, offering opportunities for preservation and growth. By understanding how trusts interact with taxes, you can ensure that your legacy stands strong and resilient against the burden of tax obligations. Remember that understanding this knowledge can help you create a tax-efficient plan to ensure that you fulfill your wishes as intended.

The journey through estate planning continues, and as the path unfolds, the focus shifts to other crucial elements of your plan. Each step builds upon the last to create a cohesive and robust strategy that honors your legacy and secures your beneficiaries' futures.

5

ESTATE STRATEGIES FOR EVERY STAGE OF ADULT LIFE

The tapestry of life is rich with individual threads, each representing a different path, a unique story. Many people believe that estate planning is only essential for those who have spouses or children, which can overshadow its significance for single adults. But the truth is, regardless of marital or parental status, every adult has a legacy—assets, decisions, and healthcare preferences—that needs a voice. This chapter highlights the often-overlooked essentials of estate planning for the single adult, mapping out strategies that affirm one's autonomy and secure one's interests.

PLANNING FOR SINGLE ADULTS

Asset Distribution

Asset distribution for the single adult isn't about dividing wealth among a spouse and offspring; it's about honoring personal relationships and supporting the causes close to one's heart. It's also about transferring assets smoothly and efficiently to avoid additional burdens on loved ones.

- Designate Beneficiaries: Review all your accounts, especially retirement plans and insurance policies, to ensure beneficiaries are updated. This simple act can prevent your assets from being tied up in probate, the legal process that can otherwise decide where your assets go if beneficiaries are not designated.
- Consider a Living Trust: A living trust can be an intelligent choice for singles. You can control your assets while alive and specify how they should be handled after you pass away. If you have a cherished collection, property, or investments, a trust can ensure they go exactly where you intend.

Guardianship Decisions

For single adults, "guardianship" may conjure images irrelevant to their life stage. However, the concept extends beyond the care of children—it also applies to your care should you become unable to make decisions.

- Choose a Proxy: Appointing a durable power of attorney for finances and healthcare ensures that someone you trust can manage your affairs if you cannot. This person can pay your bills, manage your investments, and make decisions about your medical care according to your wishes.

Healthcare Directives

Healthcare directives are your medical voice when you cannot speak. They're about making your medical preferences known and designating someone to oversee these wishes.

- Living Will: A living will is where you document your wishes regarding life-sustaining treatments. Would you want aggressive treatment for a terminal illness? What about a "do not resuscitate" order? These are tough questions, but addressing them head-on ensures your healthcare preferences are respected.
- Medical Power of Attorney: This document appoints someone to make healthcare decisions on your behalf. It complements your living will, as this person interprets and implements your wishes as medical situations arise.

Visual Element: Checklist
Estate Planning Essentials for Single Adults

- Review and update beneficiaries on all accounts.
- Consider establishing a living trust for asset management and distribution.
- Choose a reliable power of attorney for finances and healthcare.
- Create a living will to document your healthcare preferences.
- Appoint a trusted individual with a medical power of attorney.

Estate planning for single adults is less about tradition and more about personal legacy. It's a proactive stance, a declaration of independence and responsibility. Just as one might take pride in purchasing their first home solo, crafting an estate plan is a statement of self-reliance and foresight—a plan that stands as a testament to the life you've built and the relationships you've cherished.

These strategies are not one-size-fits-all; they require personalization. Tailoring a suit to fit your unique measurements is similar to customizing your estate plan to fit your life circumstances. It's about making informed, strategic decisions that reflect your current situation and anticipated future changes.

This section lays the groundwork for single adults to take charge of their estate planning. The following chapters will address the nuances of estate strategies for married couples, blended families, and unmarried partners. The intention is to ensure that each thread in the fabric of adult life weaves together with care and purpose.

ESTATE PLANNING FOR MARRIED COUPLES

In the sphere of marriage, the union of two lives extends beyond daily companionship to include the intertwining of financial and legal affairs. Estate planning within the bonds of matrimony necessitates a nuanced approach reflecting the shared life you've built and the individual legacies you contribute to that partnership. Ensuring both parties' wishes are honored, protecting their assets, and realizing the couple's joint intentions is a delicate balance.

Joint Ownership

Married couples should revisit the decision of holding assets jointly through the lens of estate planning instead of making it the default ownership mode. Joint ownership, where both spouses own the property together, can simplify the management of assets and provide a clear path of succession. However, it also means that the asset is not solely yours or your spouse's but belongs to you both legally.

- Titled Assets: Both spouses frequently hold titles for homes, vehicles, and bank accounts. This approach can offer several advantages, such as facilitating the smooth transfer of these assets to the surviving spouse without the need for probate.
- Considerations: When opting for joint ownership, it's vital to understand the implications. For instance, should one spouse encounter legal difficulties, jointly owned assets may be at risk. Additionally, if both spouses pass away simultaneously, the question of the following beneficiaries becomes paramount.

Survivorship Rights

The term "survivorship rights" is particularly resonant for married couples. It denotes the principle that upon the death of one spouse, ownership of certain jointly held assets automatically transfers to the surviving spouse. This provision in joint tenancy agreements bypasses the probate process, allowing immediate asset access.

- Joint Tenancy with Right of Survivorship (JTWROS): This form of ownership is common among married couples, ensuring that assets like real estate and bank accounts transition smoothly to the surviving spouse.
- Tenancy by the Entirety: In some states, this particular form of joint tenancy is available only to married couples, providing an added layer of protection against individual creditors of one spouse.

Tax Considerations

Taxes are an inevitable element that married couples must navigate in estate planning. The interplay between estate planning and taxation can be complex, yet strategic planning offers opportunities to minimize the tax burden on the surviving spouse and eventual heirs.

- Unlimited Marital Deduction: A cornerstone of estate tax planning for married couples, this provision allows for an unlimited amount of assets to be transferred to the surviving spouse tax-free, provided the spouse is a U.S. citizen.
- Portability: The concept of portability allows a surviving spouse to utilize any unused portion of their deceased spouse's federal estate tax exemption. This can effectively double the amount the couple can pass on without incurring estate taxes.
- Gift Splitting: Couples may elect to split gifts made to others, effectively doubling the annual gift tax exclusion amount and reducing their taxable estate without incurring gift tax.

Married couples need to execute an intricate dance in estate planning, where they harmonize individual desires with joint aspirations, and the legal framework must accommodate love and loss. When assessing how assets are held, it is important to carefully consider the surviving spouse's rights and strategically approach any potential tax implications. Engaging in this planning process is not just a financial exercise but an act of love and responsibility, ensuring the life you've built together is honored and preserved for the future.

ADDRESSING NEEDS OF BLENDED FAMILIES

In the mosaic of modern family structures, blended families reflect a rich amalgamation of past and present relationships, each with their own emotional and legal intricacies. Estate planning in this context requires a sensitive touch—a careful calibration that respects previous commitments while honoring current bonds.

Stepchildren Considerations

When families blend, stepchildren often become as dear as one's biological offspring. They may share your home and your life, yet without legal adoption; they do not automatically share in your estate. The absence of a biological link can create unintended barriers to inheritance, making intentional inclusion in estate planning documents critical.

- Explicit Inclusion in Wills and Trusts: Ensure that your stepchildren are not overlooked by naming them in your will or creating specific provisions within a trust. This act can also mitigate assumptions arising from standardized language in estate planning documents that traditionally favor biological relationships.
- Education and Trust Funds: For stepchildren, specially designated funds can provide educational opportunities or financial support that mirrors what you might set aside for biological children, ensuring equitable treatment among all children in the family.

Ex-Spouse Obligations

Navigating the obligations to an ex-spouse while balancing the needs of a current family can be akin to walking a tightrope. When you weave financial responsibilities stipulated in alimony, child support, or divorce agreements into your estate plan, you actively ensure that your financial obligations are met.

- Life Insurance Policies: Ensure your current family's security while structuring ongoing support commitments appropriately. It's a strategy that maintains the integrity of your financial obligations without disrupting the estate's distribution to other beneficiaries.
- Clear Documentation: Maintaining meticulous records of your commitments and how you address them in your estate plan is essential. This clarity can prevent future disputes and ensure all parties understand the rationale behind certain asset allocations.

Fair Asset Division

Achieving fairness in asset division within a blended family is a delicate endeavor. It is not merely a matter of mathematics but a balance of emotional equities, past contributions, and future needs.

- Prenuptial Agreements: These can be instrumental in clarifying the intentions for asset division, particularly for assets brought into the marriage. They provide a predetermined roadmap for asset allocation, which can be a valuable reference point in estate planning.
- Dynamic Trust Structures: Blended families can customize trusts to suit their specific dynamics. A marital trust, for

example, can provide for a surviving spouse during their lifetime, with the remaining assets then flowing to children from a previous marriage.

Crafting an estate plan that encapsulates the essence of a blended family requires a nuanced approach—one that considers the emotional and financial threads that bind the family tapestry. It is about creating a plan that feels just and equitable to all members, recognizing that each has played a role in the family's story.

In blended families, the estate plan becomes a narrative that weaves divergent histories into a cohesive story of unity and respect. It demands diplomacy and foresight, ensuring each member's role and rights are acknowledged and preserved. With careful planning and clear communication, the estate plan for a blended family can be a testament to the strength and love that binds its members together.

ESTATE PLANNING FOR UNMARRIED PARTNERS

In modern society, couples who are not married may face legal challenges due to the lack of recognition of their union. Estate planning for unmarried partners is crucial in affirming their commitment and ensuring that both are protected and provided for according to their mutual intentions.

Legal Protections

Unlike their married counterparts, unmarried partners cannot rely on the legal system to automatically intercede on their behalf in the event of one partner's incapacity or death. This makes establishing legal protections a priority.

- Durable Powers of Attorney: Partners can make critical decisions on each other's behalf and ensure their voices are heard when it matters most by creating durable powers of attorney for healthcare finances.
- Cohabitation Agreements: These contracts can outline each partner's rights and responsibilities, providing a semblance of the legal structure that marriage offers. They can include details on property division, support obligations, and more, tailored to fit the unique contours of the couple's relationship.

Property Ownership

Property and real estate pose particular challenges for unmarried partners, as the default legal presumptions that benefit married couples do not apply.

- Joint Tenancy with Right of Survivorship: This form of co-ownership ensures that upon the death of one partner, the property in question passes directly to the surviving partner without the need for probate. It provides a smooth transfer of ownership, reflecting the shared life the couple has built.
- Tenancy in Common: For those who wish to maintain individual ownership stakes or pass their share to someone other than their partner upon death, tenancy in common offers an alternative. A beneficiary of their choosing can receive a specified share of each partner's property.

Beneficiary Designations

Unmarried partners can ensure that the surviving partner is provided for by naming each other as beneficiaries on life insurance policies, retirement accounts, and other financial instruments.

- Payable on Death (POD) and Transfer on Death (TOD) Accounts: These designations allow unmarried partners to name each other as beneficiaries on bank and investment accounts. They are straightforward tools that facilitate the transfer of assets outside the probate process.
- Retirement Plans and Insurance Policies: Regularly reviewing and updating beneficiary designations on retirement plans and insurance policies is imperative. These designations should reflect the couple's current wishes and can be crucial in supporting the surviving partner financially.

For unmarried partners, estate planning is not an abstract concept; it's a tangible way to protect each other in a world where legal recognition of their relationship is not a given. It's a declaration that their mutual support, shared dreams, and life together are equally valid and worthy of protection as those within a marriage. With thoughtful planning and legal tools, unmarried partners can create a safety net that honors their relationship and secures their shared future.

As we close this chapter, we recognize the importance of intentionality and foresight in estate planning. Whether navigating life's path solo, alongside a spouse, within a blended family, or with an unmarried partner, the strategies and protections you put in place today serve as the framework for the legacy you'll leave tomorrow. This thoughtful preparation ensures that your wishes are not left to the winds of chance but are anchored firmly in your care and consideration for those you hold dear.

Our exploration continues, evolving with each new life change and adapting to meet the needs of every unique situation. The next chapter will further expand on estate planning principles, guiding you through the complexities and bestowing you with the knowledge to secure your legacy, no matter what the future holds.

6

SAFEGUARDING YOUR DIGITAL LEGACY

The distinction between the tangible and the intangible blurs as we increasingly live our lives online in this era. Your digital footprint, a mosaic of online interactions and assets, is as much a part of your legacy as the physical items you bequeath. Yet, regarding estate planning, these digital assets are often left in a nebulous state of oversight, floating in uncertainty. It's vital to anchor them down, ensuring they are as meticulously cataloged and managed as your material possessions.

Consider the digital world a vast ocean, with every email, tweet, or transaction a single droplet. Over a lifetime, these droplets accumulate into a personal sea of data, a digital estate that requires careful navigation. Without a map and compass—tools to define and manage your digital assets—your online life risks becoming adrift, susceptible to the currents of chance.

DEFINING DIGITAL ASSETS

Digital assets are not just bits and bytes but the repositories of our personal stories, creative expressions, and financial endeavors. Let's explore three critical categories of digital assets that, without question, should feature in your estate planning.

- Social Media Accounts Social media platforms are the 21st-century scrapbooks of our lives. They chronicle everything from momentous occasions to the daily minutiae that, collectively, tell the story of 'you.' Think of each post as a page in an autobiography you're writing in real-time. Facebook, Instagram, Twitter, and LinkedIn accounts can contain decades of personal history, connections, and insights into your interests and activities. These accounts may hold sentimental value for loved ones or serve as a record of your personal and professional legacy.
- Digital Currencies Cryptocurrencies, like Bitcoin and Ethereum, are the modern-day treasure chests. They can be highly valuable and, crucially, they're assets that exist outside traditional banking systems. Given their decentralized nature, access hinges on specific keys—passwords and codes that, if lost, render the currency as good as sunken treasure: irretrievable. Their volatile nature also means their worth can fluctuate dramatically, making timely management and transfer crucial.
- Online Businesses An online business is akin to a ship you've built and set sail in the digital ocean. It carries your entrepreneurial spirit, financial investments, and professional reputation. Whether it's an e-commerce platform, a freelance portfolio, or a digital content creation hub, this asset requires proactive stewardship to ensure its continuity or smooth transfer in your absence.

Visual Element: Infographic
Mapping Your Digital Assets

A visual representation showing the different types of digital assets and their place in your digital estate:

- Social Media Accounts: Connect the dots between various platforms to illustrate the web of your online presence.
- Digital Currencies: Depict a vault with different cryptocurrency symbols representing value and security considerations.
- Online Businesses: Show a ship navigating digital waters, symbolizing the ongoing management and potential growth of the business.

Understanding your digital assets is the first step in reining them under your estate plan's umbrella. It's about taking the nebulous and grounding it in the concrete, transforming your digital existence from a transient stream into a well-charted river that flows according to your design.

In recognizing the value of these digital assets, you begin to understand the necessity of including them in your estate plan. They are not merely ancillary components but integral parts of your legacy that require the same attention as any physical asset you own. Their management demands a proactive approach, ensuring they are not left to languish in the digital expanse but are preserved, protected, and passed on as you intend.

As we navigate the following chapters, we'll harness the tools and strategies to identify and secure your digital assets within your estate plan. Let's explore why including these assets is essential, how to inventory them accurately, and the steps required to integrate them into your estate planning with the same level of care as your physical assets.

Your digital legacy is a testament to your era—an era where the line between real and virtual is increasingly intertwined. By bringing your digital assets into the fold of your estate planning, you ensure that every aspect of your legacy—online and off—is accounted for and protected.

THE IMPORTANCE OF INCLUDING DIGITAL ASSETS IN YOUR ESTATE PLAN

Navigating the digital landscape requires foresight. You should shield your digital assets, like safeguarding a house or a family heirloom. The tapestry of our online lives, woven from emails, photos, blogs, and more, demands protection. It is not just about preventing loss; it's about ensuring that the essence of who we are, as etched into the digital realm, is preserved and that our online endeavors continue to flourish or conclude with dignity, per our wishes.

Asset Protection

Treat digital assets with the same level of vigilance as physical property since they carry both monetary and sentimental value. Investors should take online investment portfolios and revenue streams from digital platforms seriously, as they are tangible assets. Safeguarding these assets means ensuring they are not vulnerable to cyber threats or legal ambiguities. Establishing clear directives within your estate plan for how these assets are to be managed or transferred can preclude potential financial losses that might otherwise occur through oversight or mismanagement.

Privacy Concerns

In the digital sphere, privacy is paramount. Our online interactions, from communication to transactions, often contain sensitive information that, in the wrong hands, could lead to privacy breaches or identity theft. Including digital assets in your estate plan demands a strategy to protect this information. It is about delineating who should gain access to your digital life and under what circumstances. An estate plan that addresses digital assets can help maintain the confidentiality of personal data, ensuring that only designated individuals familiar with your privacy expectations can control these assets.

Legacy Preservation

The story of our lives today is told in pixels as much as in paper and ink. Digital assets constitute a narrative of our existence, capturing moments, ideas, and interactions that map our journey through life. Preserving this legacy means considering how you want your digital life handled posthumously. Will social media profiles remain as memorials, or should they be deactivated? How will personal blogs, websites, or creative works be maintained? The answers to these questions form the blueprint for preserving a digital legacy that respects your memory and reflects your life's narrative.

When you weave digital threads into your estate plan, you ensure that you capture the full extent of your assets and treat the digital manifestations of your life with the same care as the physical ones. This inclusion is not merely a precaution but a reflection of our interconnected world—where our digital presence continues to echo beyond our physical existence.

HOW TO INVENTORY YOUR DIGITAL ASSETS

In an age where our digital footprints are as significant as our physical ones, taking stock of online assets is paramount. To inventory your digital assets is to lay down the map of your online world, marking each treasure chest and noting the paths to reach them. In this meticulous process, we detail the contents of a safety deposit box, ensuring that we account for each item and know its worth.

Listing Online Accounts

The first step in taking inventory is to compile a list of your online accounts. A detailed and structured inventory must note each item and identify its specific location, similar to how a librarian catalogues books.

- Email Accounts: These are often the keys to your digital kingdom, as they can be used to reset passwords and access other accounts. Record each email address, the provider, and any notes on its primary use.
- Financial Accounts: Include banking, investment, and retirement accounts, detailing the institution, account types, and any relevant online customer IDs or usernames.
- Social Networks: List each platform where you maintain a presence, from professional networks like LinkedIn to personal ones like Facebook and Instagram.
- Online Retail Accounts: Document any sites where you shop or sell goods, including marketplaces like eBay or Etsy, and retail giants like Amazon.
- Subscription Services: Note down subscription services for entertainment, software, news outlets, and any other recurring digital service.

- Utility and Service Providers: Remember to manage accounts related to utilities, phone services, and internet providers online.

Documenting Digital Properties

Beyond the list of accounts lies the realm of digital properties that may include domains, blogs, or any other online real estate you own. These properties often hold value both in monetary and intellectual terms and should be cataloged with care.

- **Domains:** For each domain, note the registrar, expiration date, and any associated hosting services.
- **Blogs and Websites:** Document where you have hosted these files, provide details about your content management system, and specify any associated revenue streams.
- **Digital Media:** Keep a tally of your digital creations, whether photographs, videos, or written works, and where they're stored or published online.
- **Online Business Interests:** If you operate or have stakes in online businesses, record the business structure, partners, and digital assets associated with these enterprises.

Recording Access Information

A map is only as good as its ability to guide one to the destination. To ensure that you can manage your digital assets according to your wishes, you must include access information in your inventory of digital assets.

- Passwords: Store passwords securely, whether in a password manager or encrypted digital vault, and provide a means of access to someone you trust.

- Security Questions and Two-Factor Authentication: Record the answers to security questions and details of any two-factor authentication methods in place, such as a mobile device or authentication app.
- Encryption Keys: Ensure that any keys or seed phrases are securely recorded and stored for digital currencies or other encrypted assets.
- Access Permissions: Remember to detail any permissions that may be required to access certain assets, particularly if you share them with business partners or family members.

Take your time in creating a thorough inventory of your digital assets. It requires the same attention and diligence as auditing a complex financial portfolio. Each entry is a commitment to the future management of your online presence and the legacy you choose to leave behind. It's a living document, one that should evolve as your digital life grows and changes.

With every account listed, every property documented, and every piece of access information securely recorded, your digital estate stands in clear view. This clarity simplifies the management of your online assets and provides a beacon for those handling your digital legacy. Your digital inventory, with its detailed entries and careful annotations, becomes a guidebook for the stewardship of your online life, ensuring that your digital assets are as respected and maintained as the physical world you inhabit.

STEPS TO INCLUDE DIGITAL ASSETS IN YOUR ESTATE PLAN

In the meticulous task of estate planning, incorporating your digital assets ensures that the full spectrum of your estate is acknowledged and prepared for future transitions. It's about taking affirmative action to weave these assets seamlessly into the legal fabric of your will and trust while also designating a trustworthy individual as the custodian of your digital life.

Update Will and Trust

Updating your will and trust to include digital assets safeguards your online presence and ensures a smooth transition of these assets to your beneficiaries. It's an act that acknowledges the evolving nature of asset ownership and the importance of digital holdings within your estate.

- Explicit Instructions: When creating your will and trust, be clear about handling each of your digital assets. Each decision should be unambiguous, whether about continuing online business, distributing digital art collections to loved ones, or memorializing social media accounts.
- Asset Allocation: Assign each digital asset to a beneficiary or specify a trust to manage the assets. For instance, if you have a valuable online business, you could create a separate trust to manage the company's assets, providing detailed guidelines on how the business should be run or dissolved.
- Legal Compliance: Ensure that your will and trust comply with online platforms' and digital service providers' Terms of Service Agreements. Tailoring your estate plan to the terms outlined in these agreements is paramount since they often specify what can legally be done with accounts after the owner's death.

Assign Digital Executor

A digital executor is someone you appoint to manage your online presence after you pass away. This role carries significant responsibility, as it involves navigating both the technical and sentimental aspects of your digital life.

- Role Definition: Define the role of the digital executor in your will or trust, outlining their responsibilities and the scope of their authority. This person must access, manage, and close online accounts, safeguard digital assets, and execute your digital estate plan.
- Skill Considerations: Choose an individual with the necessary technical skills and understanding of digital platforms. You must find someone who respects your privacy and whom you can trust with sensitive information.
- Legal Authority: Provide your digital executor with the legal authority to act on your behalf. This text clarifies the legal right to access digital assets, including electronic communications, online accounts, and digital files, as permitted under state law and federal legislation such as the Revised Uniform Fiduciary Access to Digital Assets Act (RUFADAA).

Provide Access Instructions

Access instructions are the keys to your digital estate, offering a clear path for your digital executor to fulfill their role. These instructions should be precise, secure, and updated regularly.

- Secure Storage: Keep access instructions in a secure location, such as a safe deposit box or with an attorney, and

ensure your digital executor knows how to access them when needed.
- Detailed Access Methods: Provide instructions for accessing digital assets, including login credentials, security questions, and guidance for accessing encrypted data or devices.
- Regular Updates: Digital access credentials can change frequently. Establish a routine for updating your access instructions to reflect changes to accounts, passwords, or security features.

Don't take incorporating digital assets into your estate plan lightly. It is an essential step that demands attention to detail, foresight, and an understanding of the digital landscape. To ensure that your digital assets receive the same level of care and diligence as the rest of your estate, update your will and trust, assign a digital executor, and provide comprehensive access instructions.

As we conclude this chapter, it's clear that digital assets are as integral to our legacy as tangible property. Managing these assets effectively requires a blend of technical understanding and thoughtful planning, ensuring that our online identities and possessions are respected and transferred according to our wishes. In the next chapter, we'll shift our focus to another crucial aspect of estate planning: navigating the complexities of family dynamics and ensuring that your estate plan serves as a unifying force rather than a source of discord.

Making Estate Planning Accessible to All

"Always plan ahead. It wasn't raining when Noah built the ark."

— RICHARD CUSHING

The very concept of estate planning leaves many people running for cover, desperate to put it off for as long as they can. It's not because they don't understand that it's important. It's not because they don't care what happens after they're gone. It's because the mass of legal and financial terminology there is to sift through is like a labyrinth.

Frankly, it makes their brain hurt, and they're intimidated by the entire concept before they even get to the emotional weight of thinking about how their families will be taken care of once they're gone.

What you're getting here are the stepping stones through that maze, and it's our hope that the combination of relatable scenarios and actionable advice will give you everything you need to make this journey less daunting.

We want to bring that to as many people as possible. Estate planning is something we all have to get to eventually, and when it's done early rather than being put off until the last minute, it's a weight lifted.

You can help us do that simply by leaving your feedback online, and it won't take more than a few minutes.

By leaving a review of this book on Amazon, you'll help other people looking for guidance with estate planning (and there are many!) find the help they need.

Reviews help people find the resources they're searching for, so while it may not seem like much to you, it could make all the difference to someone else.

Thank you for your support. Now, let's get back to business!

7

NAVIGATING THE WATERS OF ESTATE TAXES

Imagine standing at the edge of a sprawling vineyard that you've nurtured over the years. Each grapevine is a financial asset; together, they form the wealth you'll eventually pass on. But as with any harvest, there's a portion owed back—to the land, in the form of care and maintenance, and to the state, through taxes. Estate taxes, often called the "death tax," are the government's share of the bounty you've accrued over a lifetime. Understanding these taxes is crucial to ensuring the fruits of your labor benefit those you intend rather than being consumed by tax liabilities.

UNDERSTANDING ESTATE TAXES

Federal Estate Tax

The federal estate tax is a levy on transferring the "estate" of a deceased person. It's calculated based on the net value of the property owned at the time of death after accounting for debts and expenses. Simply put, if your estate is worth more than a certain threshold—the federal estate tax exemption amount—your estate may owe taxes to the federal government.

- Exemption Amounts: The IRS sets exemption amounts, which have historically fluctuated. As of my knowledge cutoff in 2023, estates valued under approximately $11.7 million for individuals and $23.4 million for married couples may not be subject to federal estate taxes. It's vital to stay updated, as tax laws and exemption amounts are subject to change.
- Tax Rates: For estates that exceed the exemption amounts, the tax rates can be steep, often starting at around 18% and climbing to as high as 40% for the portion of the estate that exceeds the maximum threshold.

State Inheritance Tax

Not all states impose state inheritance tax, as it is separate from federal estate tax. The government imposes an inheritance tax on the beneficiaries of an estate according to the value of the assets they inherit. The rate and applicability vary widely from state to state, with some states collecting no inheritance tax at all. In contrast, others impose rates that can significantly dent your beneficiaries' inheritance.

- Varied Rates and Exemptions: Each state that imposes an inheritance tax sets its own rates and exemption levels. For instance, some states have lower exemption thresholds than the federal level, meaning that even if your estate doesn't owe federal taxes, it might still be liable for state taxes.
- Consider the Beneficiary's Relationship: The inheritance tax rate owed in many states can depend on the beneficiary's relationship to the deceased. Spouses are often exempt,

while distant relatives or non-relatives may face higher rates.

Gift Tax

Gift tax is the federal tax applied to transferring money or property to another person while you're still alive without receiving something of equal value in return. It's a way for the government to ensure that individuals don't simply give away their wealth before death to avoid estate taxes.

- Annual Exclusion: An annual exclusion amount allows you to give away a certain sum to any number of individuals each year without incurring gift tax. As of my last update, this amount is $15,000 per recipient per year.
- Lifetime Exemption: In addition to the annual exclusion, a lifetime exemption coincides with the federal estate tax exemption. This means you can give away a certain amount over your lifetime without owing taxes—once you exceed this amount, the gift tax kicks in.
- Direct Payments: It's worth noting that certain types of gifts, such as direct payments for someone's medical expenses or tuition, are exempt from the gift tax altogether.

Visual Element: Chart
Understanding Estate and Gift Tax Exemptions

Year

    Federal Estate Tax Exemption
    Annual Gift Tax Exclusion
    Lifetime Gift Tax Exemption

2023

$11.7 million
$15,000
$11.7 million

Understanding these taxes and their implications can be as intricate as chess; each move has consequences, and your strategy will determine the outcome. Knowing the rules is the first step, but playing the game well requires foresight and planning. Understanding how federal and state taxes will impact the family business or valuable piece of property can influence your decisions today, especially if you're considering passing them on to someone else.

Estate planning is about more than just drafting documents—it's about crafting a strategy that encompasses not only the distribution of your assets but also the preservation of your wealth against the erosive potential of taxes. Remember that understanding these taxes can equip you with better decision-making abilities that align with your financial goals and the legacy you wish to leave behind.

HOW TO MINIMIZE ESTATE TAXES

Trusts

A Cloak of Protection for Your Assets

The strategic use of trusts can serve as a shield, guarding your estate against the potential siege of taxes. Imagine fortifying your assets within an impenetrable fortress-like trust. When structured astutely, trusts can significantly reduce the taxable estate, thus easing the potential tax burden upon your heirs.

- Irrevocable Life Insurance Trust (ILIT): An ILIT is a type of trust specifically designed to own a life insurance policy. When you transfer a life insurance policy into an ILIT, the proceeds from the policy are not considered part of your estate and are, therefore, not subject to estate taxes. This can offer sizable savings, especially for estates that hover around the tax exemption threshold.
- Grantor Retained Annuity Trust (GRAT): A GRAT allows you to transfer appreciating assets to beneficiaries while retaining a right to annuity payments for a term of years. Any appreciation of the assets over a set interest rate—known as the Section 7520 rate—passes to your beneficiaries tax-free. This can be an effective tool for transferring growth potential out of your estate with little to no gift tax cost.
- Qualified Personal Residence Trust (QPRT): A QPRT enables you to transfer a personal residence to a trust while retaining the right to live there for a term of years. Post-term, the residence transfers to the trust beneficiaries, often at a reduced tax cost. The transfer freezes the value of the gift at the time of transfer rather than when the beneficiaries receive the residence, making this trust advantageous.

Each trust serves as a strategic bulwark, crafted to protect specific assets from the reach of estate taxes. Transferring assets into these trusts removes them from your estate, thereby decreasing its value and the corresponding tax liability.

Gifting Strategies

The Art of Generosity

Gifting can be a proactive tactic in estate tax reduction, allowing you to disperse portions of your wealth to beneficiaries during your lifetime, thus diminishing the taxable estate. The artistry lies in gifting assets that have the potential for significant appreciation, thereby transferring the future growth out of your estate.

- Annual Exclusion Gifting: Utilize the annual gift tax exclusion to give up to the allowable amount per recipient each year. Using this exclusion regularly allows you to transfer wealth incrementally without tapping into your lifetime gift and estate tax exemption.
- Education and Medical Expenses: Payments made directly to an educational institution for tuition or to a healthcare provider for medical expenses are exempt from gift tax. These are strategic avenues for reducing your estate while investing in the well-being and future of your beneficiaries.
- Family Loan Strategy: Lend money to family members at the minimum interest rates required by the IRS, known as the Applicable Federal Rates (AFRs). If the family member then invests that money in a way that outperforms the AFR, the excess growth is effectively transferred out of your estate.

Through gifting, you can lighten your estate tax load while enriching the lives of your beneficiaries. When executed precisely, these transfers can create immediate joy and long-term benefit for those you care about, all while adhering to an intelligent estate tax strategy.

Charitable Donations

The Legacy of Altruism

Charitable giving can be a cornerstone of estate tax minimization, offering a dual benefit of fulfilling philanthropic desires and reducing the size of your taxable estate. When you earmark assets for charity, you forge a legacy of altruism and craft an estate plan that benefits from tax deductions and exemptions.

- Charitable Remainder Trust (CRT): A CRT allows you to convert a highly appreciated asset into lifetime income. It reduces your taxable income by allowing a deduction for the charitable contribution and eliminates capital gains taxes on the sale of the asset. At the end of the trust term, the remaining assets go to the charity, reflecting your philanthropic legacy.
- Charitable Lead Trust (CLT): In a CLT, the charity receives income from the trust for a term of years, after which the remaining assets revert to you or pass to your beneficiaries. This arrangement can provide significant gift and estate tax savings, particularly if the assets in the trust appreciate beyond the IRS-assumed rates.
- Donor-Advised Funds (DAF): A DAF is a philanthropic vehicle that allows you to make a charitable donation, receive an immediate tax deduction, and recommend grants from the fund over time. It's an effective way to create a lasting impact while receiving a tax benefit upfront.

Employing charitable strategies within your estate plan serves the greater good and aligns your financial legacy with your personal values. Incorporating charitable giving into your estate can achieve a more favorable tax position, ensuring your generosity extends beyond your lifetime.

In each of these strategies—trusts, gifting, and charitable donations—the goal remains constant: to minimize the impact of estate taxes on the wealth you've worked so hard to accumulate. These approaches offer avenues to transfer your assets in ways that reflect your priorities and preserve your estate for the benefit of your heirs and the causes you champion. Using these instruments, you can sculpt your legacy and ensure that your estate reflects your life's work and enduring values.

ESTATE PLANNING AND INCOME TAXES

The realm of income taxes is a landscape every estate must traverse. As you strategize your estate plan, it's imperative to consider the assets you will bequeath and the income taxes that will continue to play a role for your beneficiaries. The nuances of capital gains tax mark the path here, as do the intricacies of retirement account distributions and the particulars of life insurance proceeds. Each element demands attention to mitigate the tax burden on your heirs.

Capital Gains Tax

- Asset Appreciation: When an asset appreciates in value and is sold, capital gains tax comes into play. This tax is applied to the difference between the purchase price, known as the 'basis,' and the sale price. Understanding the basis is crucial for beneficiaries as it determines the tax implications of selling inherited assets.
- Step-Up in Basis: One significant advantage for heirs is the 'step-up in basis' rule. This means that the valuation of an inherited asset is 'stepped up' to its fair market value at the

time of the decedent's death. Consequently, if the heir later sells the asset, the capital gains tax is calculated based on this stepped-up basis, potentially reducing the tax owed.
- Holding Periods: Differentiating between long-term and short-term capital gains can impact the tax rate. Assets held for more than a year before being sold are subject to long-term capital gains tax rates, which are generally lower than short-term rates. For inherited assets, the holding period automatically qualifies for long-term treatment, providing another layer of tax efficiency for beneficiaries.

Retirement Account Distributions

- Tax-Deferred Accounts: Retirement accounts like traditional IRAs and 401(k)s are often central to estate planning. Contributions to these accounts are typically tax-deferred, meaning taxes are only paid on the money once it is withdrawn. Beneficiaries inheriting these accounts are responsible for the taxes due upon distribution.
- Required Minimum Distributions (RMDs): Beneficiaries of retirement accounts are usually required to take minimum distributions over their lifetime. These RMDs are taxed as ordinary income, and failing to take them can result in hefty penalties.
- Roth Accounts: In contrast, Roth IRAs and 401(k)s are funded with after-tax dollars, allowing for tax-free growth and distributions. However, beneficiaries must adhere to specific withdrawal rules to maintain the tax-free status of these accounts.

Life Insurance Proceeds

- Generally Tax-Free: Life insurance proceeds are typically free from income tax when paid to beneficiaries. This attribute makes life insurance a pivotal component in estate planning, as it provides a tax-efficient means of transferring wealth.
- Estate Inclusion: While life insurance proceeds are usually income tax-exempt, they may still be included in the decedent's estate for estate tax purposes, depending on the policy ownership. Proper structuring, such as ownership through an irrevocable life insurance trust, can avoid this inclusion, thereby sidestepping the potential estate tax hit.
- Accelerated Benefits: In some cases, policy owners can access life insurance proceeds before death, known as 'accelerated benefits,' if they meet specific criteria like a terminal illness diagnosis. When planning for potential healthcare expenses, it's important to consider that these funds may be taxable depending on the situation.

Addressing these aspects of income taxes within your estate plan is not just about preparation; it's an ongoing strategy that adapts to the ever-flowing current of tax laws and rates. It requires a vigilant eye on legislative changes and a hand ready to adjust the sails to maintain course for the most tax-efficient transfer of wealth to your heirs.

Understanding the impact of income taxes on your estate is akin to planting a garden with an eye toward the seasons ahead. Just as a gardener prepares the soil and selects plants that will thrive in future conditions, so must you lay the groundwork for an estate that will weather the changing tax climate. It's a proactive approach, planting today the seeds that will grow into a robust legacy for your beneficiaries tomorrow.

Each decision made in the context of income taxes—whether to sell an asset now or later, how to manage retirement account distributions, or the best way to incorporate life insurance into your plan—is a deliberate step on the path of estate planning. It's a path that meanders through a landscape of tax implications, with each turn offering opportunities to optimize your estate's financial health. With careful planning and a clear understanding of income taxes, you can ensure that the legacy you leave is not diminished by tax burdens but is instead a testament to your life's work and foresight.

STATE-SPECIFIC ESTATE TAX LAWS

The laws of the land, particularly the states where you possess assets, color the tapestry of regulations in estate taxes. These local nuances can shape the tax landscape of your estate in significant ways, much like regional climates can influence the growth patterns in a garden. Some states mirror the federal approach to estate taxes, while others chart their own course, creating a patchwork of tax environments that can impact your estate planning.

Community Property States

In states that recognize community property, a unique set of rules applies to married couples. These rules consider all property acquired during the marriage, barring inheritances and gifts, as jointly owned. Both spouses jointly own this community property, each holding an undivided half-interest.

- Impact on Estate Tax: When one spouse passes away, the community property is effectively divided into two equal

shares. This can be advantageous for tax purposes, as only the deceased spouse's half is subject to estate tax, potentially leading to a lower estate tax liability.
- Benefits of Joint Ownership: The inherent structure of community property simplifies the transfer of assets upon the death of one spouse, often streamlining the estate administration process. However, it's vital to consider this in conjunction with your overall estate plan to ensure it aligns with your wishes and maximizes tax efficiency.

States recognizing community property include Arizona, California, Idaho, Louisiana, Nevada, New Mexico, Texas, Washington, and Wisconsin, with Alaska offering an opt-in community property system. Each has its own flavor of the law, requiring attention to detail when planning your estate.

Inheritance Tax States

A subset of states imposes an inheritance tax, which, unlike estate tax, is paid by the beneficiaries of an estate rather than the estate itself. The rate at which this tax applies can significantly influence your estate planning strategies.

- Varied Rates: Inheritance tax rates can vary widely depending on the state and the beneficiary's relationship to the deceased. Spouses are often exempt, but other close relatives may face lower rates than distant relatives or unrelated individuals.
- Strategic Planning: In states with inheritance tax, careful planning can help manage the tax impact on your beneficiaries. This might involve redistributing assets during your lifetime or using life insurance policies to

provide beneficiaries with the means to pay the inheritance tax without dipping into their inheritance.

If you reside or own property in a state with an inheritance tax, it's essential to consider how this can affect your heirs and to plan accordingly to mitigate the tax burden they may face.

No Estate Tax States

Conversely, several states have chosen not to levy an estate tax. In these states, residents can pass on their wealth without the concern of state-level estate taxation, which can simplify estate planning and administration.

- Tax Planning Simplified: Without the need to plan for state estate taxes, individuals in these states can focus on other aspects of their estate planning, such as asset protection and beneficiary designations.
- Residency Considerations: Residency becomes a critical factor for those with properties in multiple states. Establishing domicile in a state with no estate tax can be a strategic move, potentially saving a significant amount in taxes upon death.

States that do not impose an estate tax provide a favorable environment for preserving wealth for future generations. However, residents must remain vigilant about federal estate tax laws and consider how changes at the national level might affect their estate planning.

Each state's approach to estate taxation can influence the strategies and tools you employ to craft your estate plan. Like a navigator reading the stars, understanding the tax landscape in which your estate resides allows you to chart a course that ensures your assets reach their intended destination with minimal tax burden. You must combine legal knowledge with strategic foresight to align your estate plan with your state's tax laws and preserve your legacy according to your wishes.

With a firm grasp of state-specific estate tax laws, you stand ready to tailor your estate plan to the unique tax environment in which you reside. It's a process that calls for a sharp eye and a steady hand as you align your assets and legacy with the tax climates shaping their future. This understanding is a vital component of your estate planning, enabling you to ensure that your estate is a reflection of your life's work and a gift that continues to benefit your loved ones according to your intentions.

In conclusion, estate planning is akin to charting a navigational course; each decision, from the distribution of assets to the minimization of taxes, is a calculated step toward the legacy you envision. As we move forward, we'll explore how to protect against the unforeseen and the inevitable, ensuring that your estate plan stands as a testament to your foresight and care for your loved ones' future.

8

NAVIGATING THE WATERS OF HEALTHCARE DIRECTIVES

Imagine a sailor at sea, navigating through fog and tumultuous waves. The clarity of their destination is obscured, the path uncertain. This is akin to facing a medical emergency without a healthcare directive—without clear instructions, your healthcare preferences may remain shrouded in uncertainty, leaving loved ones and medical professionals to guess your course. A healthcare directive acts as a lighthouse, guiding decisions with the bright light of your wishes, cutting through the fog, and providing direction during the most critical moments.

In the maze of healthcare decisions, a directive serves as your voice when you cannot speak for yourself. It's a means of communicating and affirming your values and choices regarding medical treatment. Here, we will explore the critical elements shaping this vital aspect of estate planning.

Living Will

A living will is not about finances or who gets your cherished watch; it's about the treatments you would want—or not want—when facing a severe medical condition. It's a declaration of your healthcare preferences in situations where you may be unable to express them.

- Treatment Preferences: Details in a living will include your wishes to use life-sustaining measures such as mechanical ventilation, artificial nutrition and hydration, and other forms of medical intervention.
- End-of-Life Care: This document often outlines your desires concerning palliative care—care that focuses on comfort and quality of life, particularly when facing a terminal illness.
- Real-Life Scenario: Consider someone diagnosed with a terminal condition who has detailed their choice to forego aggressive treatments in favor of hospice care. The living will ensures that this individual's healthcare aligns with their wishes, providing dignity and respect for their choices.

Durable Power of Attorney for Health Care

The durable power of attorney for healthcare directs the following of the script, which is the living will. This document appoints someone you trust—an agent—to make medical decisions on your behalf if you're incapacitated.

- Agent Selection: Choosing an agent is a significant decision. This individual should understand your healthcare philosophy and be willing to advocate for your preferences, even under pressure.

- Scope of Authority: The document should clearly delineate the agent's decision-making power, specifying what they can and cannot do regarding your medical care.
- Where and When: It's crucial to have this document in place before any medical emergency arises. The durable power of attorney for healthcare should be readily accessible to your agent and healthcare providers, perhaps registered with a hospital or primary care physician.

Do Not Resuscitate Orders

- A Do Not Resuscitate (DNR) order is a specific instruction that tells medical professionals not to perform CPR if your heart stops or if you stop breathing. A DNR focuses on this singular, critical event, unlike a living will or a durable power of attorney for health care, which can cover a range of medical decisions.
- Clear Intent: The DNR is explicit; it leaves no room for ambiguity in an emergency. It's a decision that should be made after thoughtful consideration and discussion with your doctor, understanding the potential outcomes.
- State Regulations: DNR orders are governed by state laws, so the process for creating one varies. Generally, they require a doctor's signature and must be readily available to emergency responders, such as on a bracelet or in a visible location within your home.

Visual Element: Checklist
Healthcare Directive Essentials

- Decide on your end-of-life care preferences.
- Choose a trusted individual as your healthcare agent.
- Discuss your wishes in detail with your chosen agent.

- Draft a living will and durable power of attorney for healthcare.
- Obtain a Do Not Resuscitate order if desired, following state-specific procedures.
- Make copies of these documents and inform your agent, family, and healthcare providers of their location.

Creating a healthcare directive is a proactive step that speaks to the heart of who you are and how you wish to be cared for. It's a document that reflects your medical preferences and embodies your autonomy and respect for life. It ensures that your voice echoes in the decisions made, even when you cannot speak them aloud. With a healthcare directive in place, you provide a beacon for those navigating tough choices, offering guidance and certainty amid life's most challenging storms.

THE IMPORTANCE OF HAVING A HEALTHCARE DIRECTIVE

Medical Decision Making

Empowering others to act on your medical behalf is a profound delegation of trust entrusted to someone who understands your health-related values and desires. It's a safeguard, ensuring that the care you receive aligns with your preferences should you be unable to articulate them. The stipulations you place in your healthcare directive serve as a guiding star for this individual, illuminating the path of choices that respect your autonomy and dignity.

- Clarity in Complexity: Decisions must be made swiftly when health crises erupt with little warning. A healthcare directive provides unequivocal guidance during such

tumultuous times, outlining your preferences for procedures and interventions. It mitigates the risk of unnecessary or unwanted treatments that may not align with your values or improve your quality of life.
- Legally Supported Wishes: With the backing of a healthcare directive, your agent has a legal framework to support the execution of your choices. This legal instrument ensures that healthcare providers hear and respect your voice in discussions, regardless of your capacity to communicate.

End-of-Life Care

The dignity you maintain at the end of life is a reflection of the care you receive. It's essential to articulate your wishes for this final stage —whether it involves seeking every possible treatment or focusing on comfort and quality of life.

- Personalized Care: Each person has unique thresholds for what they consider quality of life, particularly when facing a terminal illness. You can define what quality of life means to you through a healthcare directive, whether you want to sustain life at all costs or ensure pain management and preservation of dignity.
- Specifying Desires: Within your directive, you might identify specific interventions to accept or decline, like mechanical ventilation or artificial nutrition. You can also express wishes regarding palliative care, hospice, and the environment in which you'd like to spend your final days.

Family Dispute Prevention

Families can find themselves at a crossroads without a healthcare directive, with each member bringing their own perceptions of what is best. This can lead to conflicts that strain relationships and complicate decision-making during challenging times.

- Unambiguous Directives: By clearly outlining your healthcare preferences in a legally binding document, you provide a decisive direction for your loved ones. This minimizes confusion and reduces the likelihood of disagreements among family members about the appropriate course of your care.
- Emotional Burden Alleviated: Clearly outlining the course of action relieves your family from the emotional toll of making tough decisions on the fly. It also spares them the burden of wondering if they made the right choice, providing peace in a time of grief.

By considering establishing a healthcare directive, you lay the foundation for medical decision-making that honors your personal philosophies and life choices. It's a gesture that communicates your foresight and care for those you will one day leave behind, ensuring that your health and end-of-life care are managed consistently with your wishes. This directive is a testament to your values, offering clear guidance in the face of life's most uncertain moments.

UNDERSTANDING POWER OF ATTORNEY

Power of Attorney (POA) is a legal instrument that grants one individual—the agent or attorney-in-fact—the authority to act on behalf of another—the principal—in specified financial or legal matters. It's a pivotal tool within the toolbox of estate planning, as it designates who will manage your affairs and how they will do so if you're unable to act due to incapacitation or absence. The scope of this authority can vary greatly depending on the type of POA established. Below, we explore the nuances and applications of different POAs to provide a clearer picture of their functions and importance.

Durable Power of Attorney

The term 'durable' relates to the POA's resilience; it remains effective even if the principal becomes incapacitated. This durability is crucial because it ensures that the agent's authority persists precisely when it's most needed—when the principal cannot manage their own affairs.

- Scope of Authority: Typically, a durable POA encompasses a broad spectrum of financial and legal powers, from managing bank accounts and investments to handling real estate transactions and legal claims.
- Activation: It becomes effective immediately upon signing unless stated otherwise, and it endures through the principal's incapacitation, ensuring uninterrupted management of their affairs.
- Considerations: When drafting a durable POA, it's crucial to contemplate the breadth of powers granted. With great authority comes the potential for misuse, so the chosen agent must be someone of unwavering trustworthiness.

Limited Power of Attorney

The limited POA restricts specific situations, tasks, or periods, as suggested by its name. It's a precision tool tailored for particular actions and relinquishes its authority once those are complete.

- **Targeted Functions:** While you're abroad, the agent may sell a property, manage certain accounts, or execute a financial transaction.
- **Time-Bound:** The person who creates the POA usually sets an expiration date or terminates it upon completing the task for which it was created.
- **Advantage:** Its limited nature can provide peace of mind for those who wish to grant authority for a specific purpose without handing over extensive control of their affairs.

Springing Power of Attorney

A springing POA is akin to a contingency plan—it springs into action under predefined circumstances, typically the principal's incapacitation. Those who prefer to maintain control over their affairs until a triggering event necessitates delegation can use it.

- Triggering Events: The conditions that activate a springing POA are explicitly defined, often requiring medical certification of the principal's incapacity. This ensures that the agent only assumes power when absolutely necessary.
- Delayed Activation: Unlike a durable POA that becomes effective immediately, a springing POA remains inactive until the specified conditions are met. This delay can provide a sense of autonomy to the principal but may also lead to complications or delays when urgent decisions are required.
- Clarity is Key: Given the conditional nature of a springing POA, the document must be clear about what constitutes incapacitation and how it will be determined. Ambiguities could lead to disputes or legal challenges at a time when swift action might be critical.

Each type of Power of Attorney serves distinct purposes, tailored to the principal's specific intentions and circumstances. Selecting the right POA requires careful reflection on the level of control and flexibility desired, balanced against trust in the chosen agent. It is an intricate aspect of estate planning that demands precision in its crafting to ensure that your affairs are managed according to your wishes, regardless of what the future may hold.

Implementing a POA lays the groundwork for future scenarios where hindrances may arise, enabling you to act with foresight. It provides a structured approach to safeguarding your legal and financial matters, ensuring they are in capable hands. Your predetermined directives guide the agent acting on your behalf, and the POA serves as a bulwark to protect your interests and maintain the continuity of your affairs. Whether it's the durable, limited, or springing POA, each plays a strategic role in the comprehensive planning of your estate, reflecting the depth of your preparations for the uncertainties of tomorrow.

HOW TO SET UP A HEALTHCARE DIRECTIVE AND POWER OF ATTORNEY

Selecting an Agent

When you select an agent, you give them significant power over your well-being. Therefore, you should handle their selection with great care and introspection. This individual will stand as your advocate and surrogate decision-maker should you be unable to communicate your healthcare preferences.

- Alignment of Values: Compatibility of beliefs regarding medical interventions and quality of life is essential. Engage in deep conversations with potential agents to gauge their

understanding and willingness to abide by your healthcare philosophy.
- **Resilience Under Pressure:** The role requires someone who can maintain composure in stressful situations. Assess the person's ability to navigate complex medical systems and advocate firmly for your wishes in the face of adversity.
- **Availability and Proximity:** Choosing someone readily available and within a reasonable distance is practical. Proximity can be crucial in situations where immediate decisions are required.

Document Preparation

Creating healthcare directives and powers of attorney requires precision in language and legal acumen. To ensure the accuracy and legality of your wishes, it's crucial to draft these documents carefully.

- **Professional Guidance:** Enlisting the expertise of a legal professional is highly advised. An attorney specializing in healthcare directives can offer invaluable insight into the nuances of state laws and help tailor your documents to your specific situation.
- **Incorporating Specific Wishes:** Documents should reflect all your medical preferences, from the types of life-sustaining treatments you would accept or refuse to your thoughts on pain management and palliative care.
- **Updates and Revisions:** As your health and circumstances evolve, so should your healthcare directives. Regularly review and update your documents to ensure they remain relevant and reflect your current healthcare desires.

Legal Execution

For healthcare directives and powers of attorney to hold legal weight, their execution must adhere to state-specific formalities. This final step is crucial to ensure that your carefully prepared documents are recognized and enforceable.

- Witness Requirements: Most states require the presence of one or more witnesses during the signing of these documents. These individuals attest to the signature's authenticity and the signatory's soundness of mind.
- Notarization: Some jurisdictions may also necessitate the notarization of the documents, adding an extra layer of legal validation.
- Filing with Institutions: You should file copies of the documents with your primary healthcare providers, hospitals where you may receive care, and your designated agent once you execute them. These filings ensure all relevant parties know your directives and can access them when needed.

With your healthcare directive and power of attorney, you have taken a decisive step in maintaining control over your medical and personal affairs. The agent you have chosen now has a clear roadmap to follow, reflecting your healthcare preferences and legal wishes. Your proactive approach to personal healthcare management stands as a testament, offering peace of mind that your voice will still be heard even in times when you cannot speak for yourself.

As you consider life's journey, with its inherent unpredictability, the foresight to establish these directives ensures that your wishes for healthcare and personal matters are respected and upheld. This thoughtful planning is a gift to yourself and your loved ones, providing clarity and direction in what may be challenging times ahead. With these measures in place, you can rest assured that your choices will guide future healthcare decisions, aligning with your values and preserving your autonomy.

In our next chapter, we will build upon the foundations laid here, further solidifying our understanding of estate planning as we examine the strategies and tools that can protect and manage your assets for the future.

9

GUARDIANS OF LEGACY: EXECUTORS AND TRUSTEES EXPLAINED

There's a quiet strength in the steady hands that steer the ship through the storm, a resilience in the calm voice that commands amidst chaos. These are the hands and the voice of an executor or trustee when the seas of life become turbulent. The aftermath of a loss is a storm of emotions, decisions, and legalities. An executor or trustee stands as the beacon of order, guiding the vessel of an estate through the complex waters of asset management, legal representation, and the eventual distribution that honors the decedent's wishes.

In the real world, these roles are often the unsung heroes in the narrative of estate planning. They don't merely execute tasks; they uphold a legacy, carry out last wishes, and navigate the intricate legalities that arise after a person's passing. In this chapter, we grasp the gravity of their responsibilities and the impact of their actions on those who remain.

THE ROLE OF AN EXECUTOR OR TRUSTEE

Asset Management

An executor or trustee is entrusted with the helm, managing assets with a duty of care that mirrors a captain's responsibility to their ship. This role demands an intimate understanding of the estate's holdings, from bank accounts to real estate, investments to family heirlooms. It involves safeguarding these assets, ensuring they are neither squandered nor subjected to unnecessary risk. Think of it as a financial caretaker, scrutinizing expenses, maintaining property, and making prudent decisions that preserve the value of the estate.

Legal Representation

Imagine standing before a council where every decision you make is scrutinized. An executor or trustee often finds themselves in similar situations, representing the estate in all legal matters. They must navigate a labyrinth of court proceedings, from proving the will to addressing claims against the estate. They are the voice that speaks on behalf of the deceased, a voice that must resonate with authority and knowledge of legal obligations.

Distribution of Assets

The distribution of assets is a delicate dance of honoring the decedent's wishes while adhering to legal requirements. It involves a detailed understanding of who gets what, when, and how. Executors and trustees must be meticulous, ensuring each beneficiary receives their due share, as outlined in the will or trust. They act as the hand that weaves through the tapestry of the estate, stitching together the final picture that reflects the decedent's desires.

Tax Responsibilities

The realm of taxes is a complex puzzle that executors and trustees must piece together. They are responsible for filing final income tax returns, paying any estate taxes owed, and sometimes managing ongoing tax obligations for trusts. This task requires a keen eye for detail and a comprehensive understanding of tax laws to ensure compliance and minimize the estate's tax burden.

Conflict Resolution

When disputes arise, the executor or trustee must step in as the mediator, balancing emotions with the tenets of the will or trust. They hold the compass that navigates through family disagreements and beneficiary contentions, always aiming to reach a resolution that aligns with the decedent's intentions and maintains peace among the remaining parties.

Visual Element: Checklist
Executor and Trustee Essentials:

- Accurate record-keeping of all estate transactions.
- Regular communication with beneficiaries regarding estate proceedings.
- Ensuring proper insurance is in place for properties and valuable assets.
- Overseeing the appraisal and valuation of estate holdings.
- Strategic planning for tax obligations and potential liabilities.

Understanding the multifaceted role of executors and trustees is paramount in appreciating the magnitude of their duties. They are the steadying force in a time of upheaval, the custodians of an individual's final testament. Their role is grounded in trust and laden with responsibilities that reach far beyond the mere distribution of assets. Executors and trustees safeguard one's legacy by upholding the individual's last wishes and writing the final chapters of their life story with fidelity.

In the face of grief and loss, the executor or trustee's role is to provide clarity and direction, steering the estate through the complexities of asset management, legal battles, and the distribution of wealth. They are the architects of the decedent's final plan, the hands that sculpt the lasting impression of a life well-lived, and the voice that ensures the story told is true to the author's intent.

FACTORS TO CONSIDER WHEN CHOOSING YOUR EXECUTOR OR TRUSTEE

Selecting the right individual to manage your estate is akin to finding a captain for your ship; they must possess the necessary traits to navigate through complex waters with poise and precision. This choice will reverberate through the lives of your beneficiaries and the legacy you leave behind. The following considerations are pivotal in making an informed decision, ensuring that your estate is in competent and reliable hands.

Trustworthiness

At the core of this pivotal role lies the need for unwavering trustworthiness. Your executor or trustee will have access to sensitive information and control over your assets; their integrity is paramount. You must have unequivocal confidence in their ethical standards and commitment to act in your estate's and beneficiaries' best interests. This trust stems from their track record of honesty and moral conduct in personal and professional spheres.

- A history of dependable actions and decisions in past roles or responsibilities.
- A reputation among peers for ethical behavior and upholding promises.
- Absence of any conflicts of interest that may compromise their impartiality.

Organizational Skills

The executor or trustee cannot overstate the importance of managing a multitude of tasks efficiently. They must keep impeccable records, adhere to deadlines, and coordinate various elements of estate administration. Their organizational prowess will ensure everything runs smoothly, from filing court documents to managing estate accounts.

- Proven experience in managing projects or complex tasks with multiple moving parts.
- An eye for detail and a systematic approach to tracking and documenting actions.
- The capacity to prioritize responsibilities effectively, addressing urgent needs while keeping sight of long-term objectives.

Financial Acumen

A sophisticated understanding of financial matters is a cornerstone of the executor or trustee's role. They will make decisions affecting the estate's fiscal health, from investment choices to tax filings. Their financial literacy will guide these choices, aiming to preserve and maximize the estate's assets for the beneficiaries.

- Experience with financial planning, investments, or managing budgets.
- Familiarity with tax laws and estate accounting practices.
- Ability to interpret financial statements and reports to inform sound estate management decisions.

Availability

Your executor or trustee's ability to dedicate the necessary time to manage your estate is essential. The settlement of your estate can be delayed by the time-consuming demands of estate administration and the availability of resources.

- A clear understanding of the time commitment required and willingness to fulfill the role's responsibilities.
- Current obligations, such as career and family, will not hinder their ability to manage the estate.
- Proximity to the estate's assets and the legal jurisdiction where the estate will be administered.

Emotional Stability

Managing an estate is not just a financial or legal endeavor; it is an emotional one as well. The executor or trustee may need to navigate family dynamics and make tough decisions under stressful conditions. Their emotional fortitude is as crucial as their technical skills.

- The capacity to remain composed and make objective decisions, even in emotionally charged situations.
- The strength to handle grief and loss while carrying out the duties of their role.
- Skills in communication and diplomacy to address beneficiary concerns with empathy and clarity.

As you evaluate candidates for these vital roles, consider these attributes as the compass points that will guide your decision. The right executor or trustee will balance these traits, steering your estate with the care and foresight it deserves. By appointing them, you demonstrate trust in their abilities and dedication, ensuring your final wishes are honored and respected.

THE PROS AND CONS OF CHOOSING A PROFESSIONAL EXECUTOR OR TRUSTEE

In the theater of estate management, the actors who take on the roles of executors and trustees are pivotal to the performance. Among the cast, there is an option to enlist a professional—a seasoned player who brings a particular set of skills and attributes to the stage. Like any casting choice, this decision comes with its merits and limitations. This section carefully evaluates the nuances of selecting a professional executor or trustee to manage your estate.

Expertise and Experience

Professionals in estate administration often possess a wealth of knowledge garnered from years of specialized practice. Their expertise covers a broad spectrum of necessary skills, from legal knowledge to financial acumen.

- Adept at navigating the complex maze of probate court, understanding the intricacies of tax laws, and managing investments, these professionals can apply their seasoned expertise to safeguard and optimize the estate's value.
- Exposure to a diverse array of estates equips them with the ability to anticipate issues and implement strategies that may not be apparent to a layperson.

- Their experience can be particularly invaluable in estates that involve complicated assets, such as international holdings or business interests, where specialized knowledge is paramount.

Impartiality

One of the intrinsic benefits of a professional executor or trustee is their objectivity. Free from the web of personal relationships and familial dynamics, they can make decisions aligned with the decedent's wishes and the estate's best interests.

- Making decisions without bias can prevent and resolve conflicts among beneficiaries.
- Their neutrality also protects the estate, as heirs are less likely to question or question their actions based on alleged partiality.

Time Commitment

The administration of an estate can demand an immense investment of time and attention. A professional executor or trustee is committed to dedicating the required resources to manage the estate effectively.

- Equipped with an infrastructure that supports estate management demands, they can ensure that all tasks are completed efficiently and within the necessary timeframes.
- Their focus on the estate is unwavering, unencumbered by the personal obligations that might distract a non-professional from the task.

Cost

To make an informed decision about hiring a professional, it is important to take financial considerations into account. While their services provide value, they also come at a price.

- Professionals typically charge a fee for their services, which can be a percentage of the estate's value or an hourly rate. Depending on the complexity and duration of the administration process, the estate's assets pay a substantial cost.
- For those weighing the cost against the benefits, it is essential to consider the potential for savings in other areas, such as tax efficiencies or reduced legal challenges, that a professional's expertise might afford.

Lack of Personal Connection

The professional's lack of a personal relationship with the decedent or beneficiaries can be seen as a drawback despite the benefits of objectivity.

- The professional may not possess intimate knowledge of the decedent's values or the nuances of family relationships that can be crucial in interpreting the decedent's wishes.
- Beneficiaries might perceive a professional as detached or less empathetic to their sentiments and needs, which can create a sense of alienation or dissatisfaction with the administration process.

The decision to appoint a professional executor or trustee is a balancing act, weighing the scales of expertise and efficiency against cost and personal touch. The scales may tip in favor of professional management in estates with significant complexity, size, or potential for conflict. In contrast, a trusted family member or friend may be the preferred choice for those who prioritize a personal connection and are mindful of costs.

The selection process is nuanced, requiring a careful assessment of the estate's needs and the dynamics of the beneficiaries. It is a choice that can shape the decedent's legacy and the heirs' experience. The performance of the executor or trustee, whether they are a personal or professional acquaintance, plays a critical role in settling the estate.

HOW TO APPOINT AN EXECUTOR OR TRUSTEE

Identifying the individual who will manage your estate is a task marked by its gravity. This person's role, pivotal in orchestrating the faithful execution of your final wishes, requires a selection with the utmost discernment and a formal appointment process that ensures legal validity and practical functionality.

Inclusion in Legal Documents

The starting point for appointing an executor or trustee is the explicit designation within your estate planning documents. Within your will or trust, you must name the person or institution you have chosen to serve as executor or trustee. This statement of appointment should be unambiguous, leaving no doubt about your intentions.

- A detailed provision within your will, known as the executor clause, should lay out the name of your chosen executor and any specific powers or responsibilities you wish to grant them beyond the standard scope.
- Similarly, the trust document should name a trustee, outlining the scope of their authority and any specific instructions regarding the management and distribution of trust assets.

Consent and Acceptance

Before finalizing the appointment, obtaining the consent of the individual or institution you wish to appoint is crucial. This step ensures they are willing and able to take on the role's responsibilities.

- Engage candidly with potential executors or trustees about the duties involved and your expectations for how your estate should be managed and distributed.
- Secure their formal agreement to serve in the appointed role. To ensure clarity and evidence of commitment in the event of any future disputes, the person can sign an acceptance document.

Alternate Executors or Trustees

Life's unpredictability necessitates planning for contingencies. It's wise to consider alternate executors or trustees who can step into the role if your first choice is unable or unwilling to serve when the time comes.

- Name one or more successors to the primary executor or trustee within your will or trust, specifying the circumstances under which they would assume the role.
- Ensure these alternates are also informed and have agreed to serve, understanding the duties and responsibilities they may need to undertake.

Legal Formalities

The process of appointing an executor or trustee must adhere to the legal formalities required by your state of residence. These formalities are designed to ensure the enforceable nature of your estate planning documents.

- Sign your will or trust in the presence of witnesses, as state laws dictate. The number of witnesses and additional requirements, such as notarization, can vary, underscoring the need to adhere to local statutes.
- File any necessary paperwork with the relevant court or legal entity if required by law, especially in the case of trusts, which may not go through the probate process like wills.

You lay a strong foundation for managing your estate by meticulously following these steps. The individuals or institutions you choose will carry out your wishes with fidelity and diligence, empowered and prepared to act on your behalf. The process, marked by its formality and consideration, reflects the significance you place on the stewardship of your legacy.

In the winding path of life, the roles of executor and trustee stand out as critical milestones, ensuring that your estate is a lasting tribute to your life and values. With thoughtful selection and formal appointment, these roles are entrusted to individuals or institutions capable of honoring your legacy with the respect and dedication it deserves. Shaped by careful planning, your estate becomes a beacon of your life's journey, guiding your beneficiaries toward a future you have thoughtfully crafted.

As we move forward, we carry with us the knowledge that the guardians of our legacy are well-chosen and well-prepared, ready to act in our stead and ensure that our wishes are realized. Just as a lighthouse guides ships to safe harbor, our executors and trustees will guide our estate to its intended fate.

10

CLEAR HORIZONS: THE ESSENTIALS OF COMMUNICATING YOUR ESTATE PLAN

In the tapestry of life, each thread weaves a narrative telling our decisions, values, and the bonds we share with those closest to us. When the time comes to pass on the mantle of our legacy, the clarity with which we communicate our estate plan to our loved ones can mean the difference between a seamless transition and a tangled aftermath. The heart of estate planning is in the documents and legal frameworks we construct and the conversations and understanding accompanying them.

The fabric of a well-communicated estate plan encompasses transparency, foresight, and a proactive approach to sharing information. Through candid discussions and clear directives, we can ensure that the vision for our estate is clear of doubt and misinterpretation. Through this lens of open communication, we aim to illuminate the path for our heirs, providing them with both the map and the compass to navigate the journey ahead.

THE IMPORTANCE OF COMMUNICATING YOUR ESTATE PLAN

Sharing your estate plan with your heirs and executors is akin to setting the stage before the curtain rises on a play. The rehearsal precedes the performance, ensuring each actor knows their part and the cues are clear.

- Avoiding Misunderstandings: Misinterpreting your wishes can lead to assets being allocated in ways that diverge from your intentions. Explaining the rationale behind your decisions—such as why certain assets are earmarked for charity or why a business is to remain family-owned—can preempt confusion and ensure that your reasons are understood.
- Reducing Potential Conflicts: Estate matters can often amplify underlying familial tensions. Imagine a family gathered in the living room, the air thick with unspoken questions about an heirloom or a piece of property. By discussing your estate plan openly, you can address these concerns head-on, lessening the likelihood of disputes that can arise from assumptions or rumors.
- Preparing Heirs: Informing beneficiaries about their future responsibilities or inheritances can empower them. If your son is to inherit the family business, giving him insight into your reasoning and expectations can help him prepare for the role. Similarly, if your daughter is to become the caretaker of a family vacation home, discussing this with her allows her to understand the associated responsibilities.
- Ensuring Smooth Execution: An executor who is blindsided by the complexity of their role may feel as though they've been thrust onto a stage without a script. Early communication provides them the opportunity to ask

questions and seek clarifications, ensuring that when the time comes, they can perform their duties with confidence and efficiency.

Visual Element: Checklist
Estate Plan Communication Checklist:

- Draft a summary of your estate plan that outlines key points and decisions.
- Schedule individual meetings with beneficiaries to discuss their roles and share your intentions.
- Provide executors and trustees with detailed instructions and the rationale behind key decisions.
- Organize a comprehensive list of assets, liabilities, and important contacts for easy reference.

The benefit of such openness is an estate plan that functions not just as a legal document but as a clear expression of your life's work and choices. It's a blueprint that guides your loved ones through the fulfillment of your wishes, minimizing the room for error or uncertainty. By setting the stage properly, you can ensure that the narrative of your legacy unfolds as you intended, with each heir playing their part in harmony with your vision.

In crafting your estate plan, the clarity and depth of communication you establish with your heirs are as critical as the legal structures you put in place. It's a proactive measure that honors your wishes and respects the relationships and trust you've built with those who will carry on your legacy. The conversations you initiate today are the threads that strengthen the fabric of your estate, weaving a legacy that stands the test of time and change.

STRATEGIES FOR EFFECTIVE COMMUNICATION

Open and Honest Discussions

Envision communication within estate planning not as a single event but as a series of thoughtful exchanges, each building upon the last to create a mosaic of mutual understanding. It begins with the courage to engage in open and honest discussions, laying bare the details of your estate plan to those it affects. This transparency is the cornerstone of trust and sets the tone for communication.

- Address the realities of your estate, including its limitations and the reasoning behind the distribution of assets.
- Ensure you foster an environment where you welcome questions and respond thoughtfully to concerns. This approach will help ensure that each conversation clarifies everyone's understanding of your estate plan.

Regular Updates

As life unfolds, you can actively update and modify your estate plan since it is a living document. Regularly revisiting and communicating any changes to your plan is crucial in maintaining its relevance and accuracy.

- Schedule periodic reviews of your estate plan, considering life changes such as marriages, births, or the acquisition of significant assets.
- Following each review, update your heirs and fiduciaries on any amendments, reinforcing that your estate plan actively reflects your current circumstances and intentions.

Involvement of Key Stakeholders

The tapestry of an estate plan is most vibrant when woven with the threads of input and insight from those it affects. Involving key stakeholders in the planning process acknowledges their importance and fosters a sense of collective ownership over the eventual outcomes.

- Invite contributions from heirs and executors, allowing them to express their views and preferences, which may provide valuable perspectives that enhance the overall plan.
- Engage with professional advisors in the presence of your heirs, facilitating a holistic understanding of the estate plan's mechanisms and objectives.

Use of Clear and Simple Language

Our chosen language can illuminate or obscure the path we wish others to follow. In communicating your estate plan, opt for simplicity over complexity, ensuring that the terms and conditions of your plan are accessible to all, regardless of their familiarity with legal or financial concepts.

- Eschew legal jargon in favor of plain language that conveys your wishes unmistakably and fosters an understanding that transcends legal expertise.
- When technical terms are necessary, provide clear explanations that demystify the concepts, ensuring that each heir grasps the full scope and implications of the plan.

Through these strategies, effective communication becomes the wind that propels the ship of your estate plan forward, navigating through potential misunderstandings with the compass of openness and the anchor of clarity. It is the guiding light that ensures your legacy is preserved, respected, and understood by those who will carry it forward.

HOW TO HANDLE DIFFICULT CONVERSATIONS

When the moment arrives to discuss the specifics of your estate plan, it's not uncommon for the air to grow heavy with the weight of what those conversations imply. The topics may be fraught with emotion and the potential for disagreement. In these discussions, you delve into the heart of your legacy, where a careful, empathetic approach is paramount.

Empathy and Understanding

It is crucial to approach these discussions with a genuine sense of empathy. Recognize that each person will come to the table with feelings, perspectives, and anxieties about the future. Some may grapple with mortality, while others might be concerned about perceived inequalities.

- Acknowledge their emotions and validate their experiences. A simple affirmation of their feelings can build a bridge towards mutual understanding.
- Strive to view the situation through their eyes, even if their viewpoint differs significantly from yours. This act can foster a connection that eases tensions and paves the way for more productive dialogue.

Patience

Patience must be your steadfast companion throughout these discussions. There are times when the complexity of an estate plan requires multiple explanations or when beneficiaries need time to process information and express their thoughts.

- Allow conversations to unfold naturally, resisting the urge to rush through complex subjects or to impose your sense of urgency on the proceedings.
- Be mindful that comprehension and acceptance may not occur simultaneously. Grant your heirs the space to arrive at their understanding in their own time.

Active Listening

Successful communication builds upon the bedrock of active listening. When discussing your estate plan, it becomes especially critical to not just hear but fully comprehend the concerns and questions that arise.

- Focus your attention entirely on the speaker, consciously absorbing every word and the underlying sentiments they express.
- Reflect on what you hear to ensure you understand correctly and demonstrate that you value their input. This technique can also clarify any misconceptions immediately, preventing them from taking root.

Conflict Resolution Techniques

Despite the best-laid plans, conflicts may still surface. Having a toolkit of resolution techniques at your disposal can be invaluable in navigating these choppy waters.

- Identify common ground as a starting point for discussions. Emphasize shared values and objectives that all parties can agree upon, such as the desire to honor your legacy or to maintain familial harmony.
- Encourage everyone to express their viewpoints without interruption. Enabling individuals to express their thoughts actively reduces frustration and leads to viable solutions.
- Seek solutions incorporating elements from different perspectives, crafting compromises that acknowledge and respect the diversity of opinions.
- If necessary, consider the involvement of a neutral third party, such as a mediator or family counselor, who can provide structured guidance and help steer the conversation toward a mutually acceptable outcome.

Empathy, patience, active listening, and conflict resolution contribute to a foundation of respect and care. They are the tools that can smooth the edges of tough conversations, ensuring that the dialogue remains constructive even when the subject matter is complex or sensitive. Through these intentional practices, you can effectively communicate the intricacies of your estate plan, ensuring that your wishes are conveyed and received with the clarity and compassion they deserve.

Navigating these discussions requires a balance of firmness and gentleness, as you must stand by the decisions made in your estate plan while remaining receptive to the emotional responses they may elicit. It is a delicate dance, one that asks you to lead with confidence yet be responsive to the steps of your partners. This balance makes it possible to move through difficult conversations gracefully and emerge on the other side, with relationships not just intact but potentially strengthened by the experience.

With these conversations, you lay the groundwork for a transition that respects your wishes and the needs of your heirs. You equip them with the understanding necessary to carry your legacy forward, and in doing so, you fortify the bonds that form the foundation of your family. Through carefully navigated discussions, the story of your life's work and love continues beyond the final page, reaching into the future with intention and care.

PLANNING A FAMILY MEETING

Setting the Agenda

A family meeting about estate planning is like an orchestra's rehearsal before a major performance. Every note, every rest, every dynamic shift is purposefully placed on the score for musicians to interpret. Likewise, an agenda for your family meeting acts as this musical score, providing structure and guiding the flow of discussion. It is essential to detail what topics will be addressed, from the basics of the estate plan to the roles each member might play. This agenda promises transparency and sets expectations, ensuring that no topic plays out of turn.

- Itemize key discussion points, prioritizing them so that the most critical issues receive attention first.
- Include time allocations for each topic to keep the meeting on track without rushing important matters.

- Prepare to provide background information on decisions made within the estate plan, equipping your family with the context needed to understand their significance.

Choosing the Right Time and Place

The venue and timing of a family meeting are as crucial as the content. It is akin to selecting the perfect setting for a meaningful celebration—ambiance matters. The environment should encourage open dialogue and foster a sense of safety and privacy. The chosen time should be convenient and minimal stress for all involved.

- Opt for a location free from distractions, where confidentiality can be maintained and comfort is assured.
- Schedule the meeting when participants are not likely to be preoccupied with other pressing engagements or personal stressors.
- Consider the possibility of remote attendance for members who cannot be physically present, ensuring their inclusive participation through video conferencing.

Inviting Relevant Participants

In the same way that you would carefully curate a guest list for a significant event, selecting attendees for your family meeting requires thoughtful consideration. The individuals invited should have a direct interest or involvement in the estate plan.

- Extend invitations to all beneficiaries, key family members, and any individuals named in roles such as executors or trustees.
- Include professional advisors if their presence would contribute valuable insight or clarity to the proceedings.

- Communicate the purpose of the meeting in advance, ensuring invitees understand its importance and their expected contribution.

Facilitating the Discussion

Once the family meeting commences, the role of facilitator becomes central. This task involves guiding the conversation, ensuring it remains productive and adheres to the topics outlined in the agenda. The facilitator must be adept at encouraging participation from all attendees, navigating complex emotional dynamics, and maintaining focus on the objectives of the meeting.

- Start the meeting with a clear reiteration of the agenda and the desired outcomes to orient attendees.
- Invite questions and encourage a dialogue that allows for the expression of thoughts and concerns.
- Be vigilant in steering the conversation back to the agenda if it veers off course while allowing for organic discussion that can yield valuable insights.
- Summarize key points and agreements reached during the meeting to reinforce understanding and consensus among all participants.

The success of a family meeting on estate planning hinges on meticulous preparation and the intentional creation of a constructive atmosphere. It is an opportunity not only to impart information but also to listen, to build consensus, and to reinforce the familial bonds that the estate plan ultimately serves to protect and honor.

As the meeting draws to a close, the family leaves with a clearer vision of the future, a shared understanding of the path ahead, and a collective commitment to uphold the legacy entrusted to them. It is crucial to maintain unity and clarity to ensure that the estate plan truly represents the family's spirit and letter.

As we conclude each family meeting, we strengthen the threads that bind the fabric of our shared story. Each voice heard, each question answered, and each concern addressed adds depth and texture to understanding our legacy. This delicate and deliberate process is a testament to the care and love that shapes our family's narrative, ensuring that as we move forward, we do so with a collective commitment to honor and preserve the story we have woven together.

11

KEEPING YOUR ESTATE PLAN CURRENT AND RELEVANT

Imagine a garden through the seasons: in spring, it burgeons with fresh blossoms; in summer, it flourishes with vibrant greenery; as autumn arrives, leaves turn gold and fall, and when winter casts its chill, the landscape rests, awaiting renewal. Much like this garden, your estate plan must adapt to the ever-changing seasons of your life, accommodating growth, loss, and transformation.

We live in a world that is not static, and our circumstances echo this dynamism. Once aligned perfectly with your life's framework, an estate plan may become disjointed as new financial, familial, and legal climates emerge. It's natural to periodically tend to your estate plan, ensuring it remains a true reflection of your current situation and continues to serve your intentions effectively.

WHEN AND WHY TO UPDATE YOUR ESTATE PLAN

Changes in Financial Situation

Wealth is not constant; it ebbs and flows with the tides of our personal and professional lives. A promotion at work, a profitable investment, or the sale of a property can substantially alter the financial landscape of your estate. Conversely, a downturn in business, a market crash, or unexpected medical expenses can reduce the assets you once planned to bequeath.

- What: Reassessing the distribution of assets in your estate plan may be necessary to accommodate shifts in your financial situation.
- Why: To ensure your estate plan aligns with your current financial capabilities and continues to support your long-term goals.
- How: Consult with financial advisors to evaluate the impact of economic changes on your estate and adjust your plan accordingly.

Changes in Family Structure

Just as new branches grow and old ones shed in a family tree, our family structures are subject to change. Marriages, divorces, and the reconfiguring of family units necessitate updates to an estate plan to reflect these new realities.

- What: Updating beneficiaries, guardianships, and other provisions to account for changes in family dynamics.
- Why: To prevent outdated allocations from causing familial tensions and to ensure your estate plan benefits the right

individuals.
- How: Review beneficiary designations, trustees, and guardians, making changes in your legal documents to match your current family structure.

Changes in Estate Laws

Laws governing estates are as susceptible to change as the leaves in our proverbial garden. Legislators can shift legislation, tax authorities can rewrite laws, and changes can make a once-tax-efficient strategy obsolete overnight.

- What: Adjust your estate plan to adhere to new laws and benefit from beneficial legal environments.
- Why: Compliance with current laws is essential to avoid penalties and maximize your beneficiaries' benefits.
- How: Stay informed on estate law changes through professional legal counsel and adjust your estate planning strategies as needed.

Periodic Review

Regularly reviewing your estate plan is akin to seasonal pruning; it's a way to maintain the health and vitality of your estate intentions. Life can veer in unexpected directions, and your estate plan should be flexible enough to accommodate these deviations.

- What: Scheduling routine check-ups of your estate plan to ensure it remains current and comprehensive.
- Why: To catch any discrepancies or areas needing refinement, ensure your estate plan is always ready for implementation.

- How: Set calendar reminders for an annual review or tie reviews to significant dates, such as the end of the fiscal year, ensuring consistent oversight.

Visual Element: Checklist
Estate Plan Update Checklist:

- Financial Review: Assess the value of current assets and liabilities.
- Family Changes: Note any additions or reductions to the family unit.
- Legal Updates: Keep abreast of estate law changes that may impact your plan.
- Professional Consultation: Schedule annual meetings with your estate planner or attorney.
- Document Revisions: Adjust wills, trusts, and other related documents.

By incorporating these practices in your estate planning, you guarantee that your wishes will be executed precisely as you envision, regardless of life's inevitable fluctuations. It's a commitment to the stewardship of your legacy, a promise to those you love that you've considered the many facets of change and have planned for their well-being with foresight and care.

Updating your estate plan is not just an exercise in legality; it is an act of love and responsibility. You actively ensure that your legacy is not left to chance but rather shape it according to your evolving life story. Your estate plan is the soil from which your legacy will grow long after you've gone, and its cultivation is a testament to your commitment to nurturing the future of those you hold dear.

COMMON LIFE EVENTS THAT REQUIRE AN UPDATE

Marriage or Divorce

The union or dissolution of a marriage is more than a change in relationship status; it's a significant event that necessitates a fresh look at your estate plan. The entry or exit of a spouse can drastically alter the distribution of your assets and your plans for the future. In the glow of weddings, adding a spouse as a beneficiary in your will or as a joint tenant in property ownership often becomes a priority. Similarly, divorce calls for an urgent revision to remove the former spouse from holding roles or benefits they were previously assigned. This process may involve:

- Adjusting Beneficiary Designations: Life insurance, retirement accounts, and other payable-on-death accounts may need updates to reflect your current marital situation.
- Revising Legal Titles and Deeds: Ownership documents for real estate and other significant assets should be reviewed and amended to reflect your marital status.
- Renegotiating Estate Plans: Post-nuptial agreements or modifications to pre-existing prenuptial agreements might be necessary to clarify how assets should be treated within the estate.

Birth or Adoption of a Child

Welcoming a child into your family is a time of joy and anticipation as you imagine the life and opportunities you hope to provide them. It's also a moment that calls for your estate plan to evolve as you consider the future security of this new family member. You may need to:

- Designate Guardians: Should something happen to you, deciding who will raise your child is paramount. This choice should be legally documented to ensure your child's care aligns with your wishes.
- Create or Update Trusts: Establishing a trust can help manage the inheritance you leave for your child, stipulating how and when the assets will be used, such as for education or personal development.
- Secure Their Future: Life insurance policies may need adjustments to provide adequate coverage for your child's upbringing and educational needs.

Death of a Beneficiary or Executor

The passing of someone designated in your estate plan as a beneficiary or executor is a profound and saddening event. Consider addressing the void in your plan promptly. The following steps involve:

- Reallocating Inheritances: Assets destined for a deceased beneficiary need redirection, perhaps to alternate beneficiaries or through a reevaluation of your estate's distribution.
- Selecting New Fiduciaries: If an executor or trustee has passed away, identifying a new individual or institution to fulfill these duties is crucial to maintaining the integrity of your estate's management.
- Appraising Impact on Trusts: If the deceased was a trustee or a beneficiary of a trust, reviewing the terms of the trust is necessary to determine how their role and benefits should be reassigned or managed going forward.

Acquisition or Disposal of Significant Assets

The ebb and flow of your portfolio—be it the acquisition of stocks, the purchase of real estate, or the sale of a business interest—reflects the dynamic nature of your asset base. These transactions have a ripple effect on your estate plan, requiring adjustments that may include:

- Updating Asset Lists: Ensure all newly acquired assets are included in your estate plan and that any disposed assets are removed to prevent confusion or disputes during the execution of your estate.
- Evaluating Tax Implications: Acquiring or disposing of assets can have significant tax consequences. Analyzing these transactions with the help of a tax professional ensures your estate plan remains tax-efficient.
- Redefining Distribution Plans: New acquisitions warrant redistributing your assets among your heirs. In contrast, the disposal of assets could necessitate adjustments to planned bequests to account for the change in your estate's value.

In light of these life events, which can arrive on our doorsteps without a moment's notice, maintaining a responsive and up-to-date estate plan is not just a strategic move—it's an act of caring for those you hold dear. It ensures that through all of life's transitions, your estate plan stands as a steadfast declaration of your wishes, ready to support and protect your loved ones no matter the circumstances.

REVIEWING AND UPDATING YOUR WILL AND TRUSTS

Revisiting Beneficiaries

Relationships ebb and flow in the continuous flow of life, and the individuals you once placed at the forefront of your bequests might shift positions. This alteration isn't solely about preference changes; it also reflects the natural progression of life's events: marriages, births, and the unfortunate passing of loved ones. Hence, a meticulous reassessment of your beneficiaries is not merely advisable but necessary. It guarantees that you bestow the fruits of your labor upon the people you select and that no unintended consequences arise due to outdated designations.

- Scrutinizing your current list of beneficiaries should be approached with a clear mind and the latest information about each individual's circumstances.
- Consider the implications of each beneficiary's current life stage and financial needs, which may have transformed since your last estate plan review.
- Assess the impact of contingent beneficiaries and whether they still align with your objectives if primary beneficiaries cannot assume their roles.

Updating Asset Distribution

Update the blueprint for passing on your assets as your wealth fluctuates. Regular revisions ensure that your current financial landscape is mirrored accurately in your estate documents.

- Examine each asset's role and relevance within your estate, pondering whether specific allocations still serve your intended purpose.
- Factor in any changes in the value of your assets that could affect the equitable distribution among your beneficiaries.
- Be especially attentive to items of sentimental value or family heirlooms that may require special consideration to maintain family harmony.

Changing Executors or Trustees

The individuals you have entrusted with the execution of your will and the management of your trusts hold significant power in shaping the posthumous narrative of your legacy. They must remain individuals who are not only capable but also willing to undertake such responsibilities.

- Reevaluate your choices for executors and trustees, considering their availability, capacity, and willingness to serve.
- When an executor or trustee may no longer be the best choice due to changes in their life circumstances or your relationship with them, seek alternative candidates better suited to the role.
- Ensure a smooth transition of responsibilities by communicating any changes to all parties involved, including any new appointees and your legal counsel.

Addressing New Assets or Liabilities

As your estate evolves, so might the nature of your assets and liabilities. The acquisition of new property, the start of a business venture, or the incurrence of debt all play critical roles in the composition of your estate. Attending to these changes is essential to maintaining the validity and effectiveness of your will and trusts.

- Integrate any new assets into your estate plan, considering their implications for your overall asset distribution strategy.
- Evaluate how the addition of liabilities might affect the inheritance you leave behind and make provisions to address these debts through your estate.
- Update your will and trusts to reflect new assets or liabilities, ensuring each document represents your current estate.

Maintaining your will and trust is akin to keeping a cherished heirloom—requiring attention to detail, regular care, and timely adjustments. By carefully managing this legacy, you can make your vision a lasting tribute to your planning and commitment.

UPDATING YOUR HEALTHCARE DIRECTIVE AND POWER OF ATTORNEY

Health and personal wishes are the ever-shifting sands upon which we construct some of the most critical elements of our estate planning. Your healthcare directive and power of attorney represent you, speak on your behalf when you are unable to, and execute decisions based on your wishes when you cannot do so. As such, they must evolve as you do, mirroring changes in your health status and personal wishes, ensuring that your healthcare proxy and the powers you have granted remain apt and aligned with your current desires.

Changes in Health Status

With time, your health may transform in unpredictable ways. An agile healthcare directive must adapt to these shifts. A diagnosis, a significant improvement, or a gradual change in your capabilities may necessitate a reevaluation of your healthcare directive to ensure it accurately reflects your current health situation.

- Revisit the conditions and treatments your healthcare directive covers and adjust it to address any new health concerns or changes in your medical condition.
- If your health has improved significantly, certain directives may no longer be relevant and could be revised to reflect your current state of well-being.
- In the event of a decline in health, including more detailed instructions regarding your care preferences and end-of-life decisions may be prudent.

Changes in Personal Wishes

Your thoughts about healthcare choices might evolve as you navigate life's seasons. What once seemed a clear-cut decision may now present itself in a different light, colored by experience, relationships, or shifts in your values.

- Periodically reflect on your existing healthcare directive to ensure it still resonates with your present-day values and wishes.
- Consider how changes in your personal life, such as new relationships or experiences, might influence your thoughts on treatments and interventions.

- Update your healthcare directive to capture any new desires, whether they pertain to life-sustaining measures, pain management, or other medical care priorities.

Updating Healthcare Proxy

The person you have appointed as your healthcare proxy or agent is responsible for making healthcare decisions on your behalf, and their ability to fulfill this role might change over time.

- Assess whether your chosen healthcare proxy is still the best representative for your healthcare decisions, considering their current circumstances, relationship with you, and ability to carry out your wishes.
- Select a new proxy better suited to advocate for your healthcare preferences if needed. This might be due to geographical proximity, changes in your relationship, or the proxy's health.
- Communicate any changes to your healthcare proxy to your family and healthcare providers to avoid confusion should the directive be enacted.

Reviewing and Updating Powers Granted

The power of attorney you have established provides someone you trust with authority over certain aspects of your life, from financial matters to legal decisions. As your situation changes, so might the scope of the authority you wish to grant.

- Take stock of the powers you have assigned through your power of attorney and adjust them to better fit your current requirements and comfort levels.

- If your power of attorney is springing—set to activate under certain conditions—ensure that the terms of activation are still relevant to your current health and circumstances.
- Provide your attorney-in-fact with updated instructions to reflect any changes in the scope of their authority and ensure they are prepared to act in accordance with your current wishes.

In adapting these crucial documents to the flow of life's currents, you maintain their integrity and capacity to function as intended—protecting your well-being and upholding your autonomy. Through these updates, you wield control over how you will be cared for and who will manage your affairs, reflecting the person you are today and the care you wish to receive.

Guided by the knowledge that life is neither static nor predictable, keeping your healthcare directive and power of attorney up to date is an ongoing task that underscores your commitment to personal autonomy and thoughtful care. The steps you take to ensure these documents remain relevant reflect your diligence and desire to provide clear instructions that can ease the burden on those you entrust with your care and your affairs.

With this chapter, we've navigated the essential updates to your healthcare directive and power of attorney, equipping you to control your personal and healthcare decisions. As we look ahead, remember that these updates are more than mere tasks on a checklist; they are affirmations of your life's narrative, ensuring it continues to be authored by you for every page that remains.

12

ADAPTING TO THE DIGITAL FRONTIER IN ESTATE PLANNING

In the ever-evolving landscape of our digital lives, estate planning has transcended the confines of paper and ink. We live in a time where our digital footprints are as substantial—and sometimes more intricate—than the physical trails we leave behind. The digital realm is vast, encompassing everything from the tweets we send to the online portfolios representing our financial acuity. This chapter is your guide through the digital thicket, illuminating how technology reshapes the way we plan for the future.

The fusion of technology and estate planning is not a wave of the future—it's the surf we're riding now. Digital assets, online wills, and virtual tax filings are the new normal. It's not just about being current; it's about being prepared in a world where digital assets can be as valuable as tangible ones. Let's peel back the layers of the digital onion to understand how technology weaves into the fabric of modern estate planning.

Digital Assets

Our lives are increasingly online, from social media accounts to cryptocurrency investments. Digital assets are unique because they often exist in a realm that's not entirely ours to control. Consider your social media profiles—repositories of memories and connections—or your online business, which might be your primary source of income. Even your digital music library has value. These assets require special consideration for several reasons:

- Access and Ownership: Unlike physical assets, digital ones are often governed by service agreements, not by simple ownership rules. Who can legally access your Facebook account after you pass away?
- Financial Worth: Online businesses or domain names can carry significant economic value. How do you ensure they fall into the right hands without exposing them to security risks?
- Sentimental Value: Photos stored in the cloud or an email history can hold immense sentimental value for loved ones. How do we pass on these new types of heirlooms?

Online Wills and Trusts

Creating legally binding documents online replaces the traditional image of signing a will in an attorney's office. The advantages here are convenience, speed, and often lower cost. But with these benefits come new considerations:

- Validity and Legality: Ensuring that an online will or trust is legally valid in your state is crucial. Are e-signatures accepted? What about witnesses?

- Security: The digital creation of such sensitive documents requires robust security measures. How do you protect your personal information from cyber threats?
- Updates: Online platforms can make updating your documents more manageable, but they also require vigilance to ensure that changes are legally sound.

Digital Estate Management

Managing a digital estate is a task for the tech-savvy. It involves understanding your digital assets and how to access and control them. Consider the potential complexity of managing:

- Cryptocurrency Holdings: The volatile nature of cryptocurrency means that the value of these assets can change drastically. Who manages it, and how can they access it?
- Digital Rights: Intellectual property, like a blog or a digital art collection, requires careful handling to maintain its value and legal standing.
- Online Accounts: Ensuring continuity or closure of various online accounts requires detailed knowledge of each platform's policies and procedures.

Online Tax Filing

Estate taxes don't escape the digital transition. Filing taxes online can streamline the process, offering real-time updates and electronic record-keeping. Here's what to consider:

- Electronic Records: Keeping digital records of tax filings and associated documents is efficient but requires careful organization and backup.

- Regulatory Compliance: To ensure compliance, online tax platforms must stay abreast of changing tax laws. How often are these updates, and how transparent is the platform about them?
- Digital Footprint: Your online tax filings leave a digital trail that needs protection. What measures are in place to secure your estate's financial data?

The digital realm has expanded the horizons of estate planning, but it also requires us to become adept navigators of this new world. The following sections will explore the tools and services to help you chart this territory, ensure your digital advisors are steering you right, and inform you of legal changes in the digital age.

Visual Element: Infographic
Understanding Your Digital Assets:

- Social Media: Accounts on Facebook, Instagram, Twitter, etc.
- Financial: Online banking, PayPal, Venmo, investment accounts.
- Cryptocurrency: Wallets, exchanges, portfolio trackers.
- Intellectual Property: Domain names, copyrighted materials, digital art.
- Personal: Email accounts, cloud storage, digital journal apps.

In the following sections, we'll further explore the tools and strategies that can aid you in managing these digital assets effectively and securely. We'll also consider how online legal services can simplify creating and updating your estate planning documents and how to stay informed in an age where the only constant is change.

ONLINE TOOLS FOR ESTATE PLANNING

Estate Planning Software

In the quilt of estate planning, each patch—be it a will, trust, or healthcare directive—plays a crucial role in the final design. Estate planning software emerges as an invaluable needle, stitching together these elements precisely and efficiently. This software provides templates and guided workflows that simplify the creation of complex documents. They often feature:

- Interactive checklists that ensure no critical component is overlooked.
- Customizable templates that cater to individual needs and state-specific laws.
- Financial calculators that aid in assessing asset distribution and tax implications.

When used effectively, this software can simplify planning, allowing individuals to create legally binding documents without incurring high attorney fees. However, selecting a program that offers regular updates is vital to staying abreast of legal changes and ensuring your estate plan remains valid and enforceable.

Online Legal Services

The digital age has paved the way for many online legal services that democratize access to estate planning. These platforms offer a spectrum of services, from basic document generation to more comprehensive estate planning solutions. They typically feature:

- User-friendly interfaces that guide individuals through the process of document creation.
- Access to a network of legal professionals for personalized advice and document review.
- Secure cloud storage options for easy access and sharing of estate planning documents.

These services can be particularly advantageous for those with straightforward estates. They provide a cost-effective means to create essential estate planning documents while offering flexibility to consult with attorneys for more complex scenarios.

Digital Asset Management Tools

The digital realm is teeming with assets that require meticulous oversight. Digital asset management tools rise to the occasion, offering a centralized location to monitor everything from online accounts to digital currencies. These tools often provide:

- Secure inventories of digital assets, complete with login credentials and access instructions.
- Automated alerts for changes in asset values, especially pertinent for volatile investments like cryptocurrency.
- Encrypted protection for sensitive information, ensuring that details of digital assets are shielded from unauthorized access.

Adopting these tools into your estate planning ensures that digital assets are accounted for and managed with the same level of care as physical ones. They facilitate a seamless digital wealth and online presence transition to your designated beneficiaries.

Online Document Storage

Like a vault that safeguards treasured possessions, online document storage is the guardian for your estate planning documents. These digital repositories offer robust security and accessibility, ensuring critical information is safe and readily available. Features often include:

- Encryption and multi-factor authentication to protect against unauthorized access.
- Cloud-based platforms that allow for document access from anywhere at any time.
- Sharing capabilities that enable designated individuals, such as executors or family members, to access documents when necessary.

Incorporating online document storage into your estate planning creates an enduring archive of your most important documents. This digital vault becomes a cornerstone of your estate plan, ensuring that your carefully crafted documents are within reach for those who need them when the time comes.

Through the thoughtful application of these online tools, estate planning is no longer confined to dusty file cabinets and stoic lawyer's offices. Instead, it unfolds in a space where efficiency meets security, where the complexities of legal preparation meet the simplicity of modern technology. The result is an estate plan that reflects not only your earthly possessions but also your digital existence—a complete portrait of your life in the twenty-first century.

THE ROLE OF DIGITAL ADVISORS AND ONLINE LEGAL SERVICES

In an age where screens have become gateways to services once bound to the constraints of office hours and geography, the emergence of digital advisors and online legal services has redefined the estate planning landscape. This shift has broadened access and injected flexibility and personalization into a traditionally perceived rigid and daunting domain.

Virtual Consultations

In a world where face-to-face meetings are no longer a prerequisite for meaningful interaction, virtual consultations stand at the forefront of estate planning innovation. These digital meetings break down geographical barriers, enabling you to engage with legal experts regardless of location. This format is particularly advantageous for those who find mobility challenging or live in remote areas.

- Using secure video conferencing platforms ensures privacy and confidentiality, mirroring the sanctity of in-person attorney-client interactions.
- Scheduling flexibility allows discussions beyond traditional office hours, accommodating the busy lifestyles of today's clientele.
- The immediacy of virtual meetings can expedite decision-making processes, allowing for more dynamic estate planning.

The infusion of virtual consultations into estate planning is a testament to the adaptability of legal services, ensuring expert guidance is only a few clicks away.

Automated Document Preparation

The rise of automation in document preparation heralds a new era of efficiency. Automated systems can now generate complex legal documents with a precision that rivals seasoned professionals. This technology is reshaping the way estate plans are drafted:

- Algorithms tailor documents to individual needs by analyzing responses to targeted questions, ensuring a customized approach to each unique estate plan.
- Automating routine drafting tasks reduces the potential for human error, enhancing the accuracy of the final documents.
- The speed at which these automated systems operate significantly reduces the time traditionally required to draft estate planning documents.

Automated document preparation has emerged as a boon for those seeking to streamline the estate planning process, providing a fast and reliable alternative to manual drafting.

Online Legal Advice

The proliferation of online legal advice platforms has democratized access to legal expertise. These digital portals offer a wealth of information and direct counsel from qualified professionals, making legal advice more accessible than ever before.

- Interactive tools, such as chatbots and Q&A forums, provide immediate responses to pressing legal inquiries, offering guidance at the touch of a button.

- Subscription-based models allow for ongoing access to legal advice, creating a continuous support system throughout the estate planning process.
- The breadth of expertise available online ensures that you can find specialized advice tailored to the intricacies of your estate situation.

Online legal advice services have effectively opened the floodgates to legal knowledge, empowering individuals to make informed decisions about their estate plans confidently.

Digital Estate Planning Resources

The internet provides digital estate planning resources, from informative articles to comprehensive guides. These resources serve as a beacon for those navigating the complexities of estate planning.

- Online libraries collate a vast array of estate planning literature, offering insights into every facet of the process.
- Interactive estate planning checklists guide individuals through the preparatory steps, ensuring all critical components are addressed.
- Educational webinars and video tutorials provide visual and auditory learners with a dynamic approach to understanding estate planning concepts.

The wealth of digital resources available to individuals today supports a self-directed approach to estate planning. This empowerment through knowledge equips you with the understanding necessary to actively shape your legacy in the digital age.

The seamless integration of these digital services into the fabric of estate planning marks a pivotal shift in how we prepare for the future. They offer a blend of convenience, personalization, and accessibility that was once unfathomable. As we continue to embrace these digital tools and platforms, the scope of estate planning expands, transforming it into a process that is not only more efficient but also more attuned to the individual needs of each person. With the digital world at our fingertips, creating a comprehensive and personalized estate plan is no longer a distant possibility but an immediate reality.

STAYING UPDATED WITH LAW CHANGES IN THE DIGITAL AGE

Navigating the currents of legal change in estate planning can seem like charting a course through uncharted waters. Laws evolve, sometimes subtly, other times dramatically, impacting how estate plans are constructed and maintained. In the digital age, staying abreast of these changes is less about trawling through dense legal tomes and more about engaging with a flow of information that is as dynamic as it is pervasive.

Online Legal Updates

Legal websites serve as beacons, signaling shifts and trends in legislation that could affect your estate plan. A subtle alteration in tax law or a new ruling on digital asset inheritance could ripple through your arrangements, necessitating updates.

- Subscription services alert you to relevant legal changes, with experts translating legalese into actionable intelligence.
- Interactive forums allow for real-time discussions with professionals and peers, fostering a community approach to understanding and adapting to new laws.

Digital Newsletters and Blogs

In the vast expanse of the internet, newsletters and blogs act as compasses, guiding you towards relevant updates. Curated by legal experts, these periodic publications offer insights into the implications of recent changes and provide foresight into anticipated legal trends.

- Newsletters from esteemed law firms or legal thought leaders present condensed, insightful summaries of recent developments.
- Blogs often explore the practical application of legal changes, offering scenarios that could mirror your estate planning considerations.

Webinars and Online Courses

Webinars and online courses are the classrooms of the digital world. They offer structured learning from estate planning and law experts, often focusing on the latest legislative changes and their implications.

- Interactive webinars provide opportunities to pose questions directly to legal experts, gaining clarity on complex issues.
- Online courses on legal platforms offer in-depth explorations of specific topics, allowing for self-paced learning to deepen your understanding of changes that affect your estate plan.

Social Media Channels

Social media has become a vibrant tapestry of information sharing. Legal professionals, law firms, and industry organizations often broadcast updates and insights on these platforms.

- Following reputable legal entities on platforms like LinkedIn or Twitter can provide steady updates and professional interpretations.
- Engaging with content shared by legal professionals can lead to a deeper understanding of law changes and foster a network of resources for future inquiries.

The digital age has transformed staying informed from passively receiving information to an active pursuit. With tools and platforms designed to streamline knowledge acquisition, adapting your estate plan to the latest legal changes is a process marked by efficiency and engagement. The key lies in selecting the proper channels that resonate with your needs and preferences and integrating their use into your routine. Doing so ensures that your estate plan remains robust and responsive to the legal landscape, reflecting your wishes and the latest in legal compliance.

Staying informed is a perpetual endeavor, yet it need not be overwhelming. The digital age has provided us with many channels through which we can receive updates, engage with experts, and educate ourselves on the intricacies of estate planning law. This chapter has illuminated the resources available to keep your estate plan in harmony with the law's evolving tune. By embracing the digital tools at our disposal, we ensure that our planning remains current and relevant.

As we close this discussion, we focus on the horizon, where the principles of estate planning intersect with the practicalities of implementation. The journey continues as we apply the knowledge we've gained, crafting legally sound and deeply personal plans, reflecting our values and the legacies we aspire to leave behind.

Ready to Be an Inspiration?

It's no small feat to get your affairs in order: Take a moment to be proud of taking this step, and inspire others to join you.

Simply by sharing your honest opinion of this book and a little about your own experience, you'll show new readers where they can find all the estate planning guidance they need.

WANT TO HELP OTHERS?
LEAVE US A REVIEW TO BENEFIT OTHERS JUST LIKE YOU

Thank you so much for your support. It makes more of a difference than you realize.

CONCLUSION

As we draw the curtain on this journey through the intricacies of estate planning, you have traveled with me from the foundational aspects of wills and trusts to the nuances of healthcare directives and digital asset management. Together, we've charted a course through the sometimes turbulent, often complex, but always vital seas of securing your legacy.

Remember that estate planning involves much more than completing a simple checklist of tasks. By engaging with each chapter, you've empowered yourself with knowledge, turning what might once have seemed like a maze of legalese into a clear path forward.

The empowerment of informed estate planning cannot be overstated. It offers peace of mind, not just for you but also for those you hold dear. By taking the reins of your estate plan, you've stepped into a role that safeguards your future and honors your past. You've learned the significance of keeping your documents current, adapting to life's inevitable changes, embracing the digital revolution, and transforming how we think about our assets and legacies.

Now, I invite you to take the critical next step:

1. Secure your legacy.
2. Reflect on the strategies that resonate most with your life's narrative. Whether you're just starting or revisiting an existing plan, the moment to act is now.
3. Gather your documents, consult with professionals if needed, and ensure that your estate plan is a living, breathing reflection of your values and wishes.

The estate planning journey is unique for each of us, woven with individual threads of our experiences and dreams. Your estate plan is a testament to your life's work, a narrative crafted with intention and foresight. As you continue to write this story, remember that it's not just about the assets you leave behind but also the memories and the legacy that echo through generations.

In closing, I am grateful to you for allowing me to guide you through this process. Remember that estate planning is not a solitary endeavor but a bridge built on the pillars of community, guidance, and mutual support. As you move forward, know that you are not alone on this path. Your courage to face this essential aspect of life head-on is a profound act of responsibility and love.

Secure your legacy, embrace the future, and may your estate plan stand as a beacon of your dedication to those you love and the life you've lived.

REFERENCES

- *What Is Estate Planning? Definition, Meaning, and Key ...* https://www.investopedia.com/terms/e/estateplanning.asp#:
- *10 Risks or Consequences for Not Having an Estate Plan* https://jackrobinson.com/10-risks-or-consequences-for-not-having-an-estate-plan/
- *Steps to Create an Estate Plan* https://www.consumerreports.org/cro/2013/11/how-to-create-a-bulletproof-estate-plan/index.htm
- *How to Prepare for Upcoming Estate Tax Law Changes* https://www.kiplinger.com/retirement/estate-tax-law-changes-how-to-prepare
- *Executor Of Estate: Definition And Duties* https://www.quickenloans.com/learn/executor-of-estate
- *Power of Attorney (POA): Meaning, Types, and How and ...* https://www.investopedia.com/terms/p/powerofattorney.asp
- *Glossary of Estate Planning Terms* https://www.americanbar.org/groups/real_property_trust_estate/resources/estate_planning/glossary/
- *Probate: What It Is and How It Works With and Without a Will* https://www.investopedia.com/terms/p/probate.asp
- *Wills — Legal Requirements & Limitations - Justia* https://www.justia.com/estate-planning/wills/
- *Introduction to Wills* https://www.americanbar.org/groups/real_property_trust_estate/resources/estate_planning/an_introduction_to_wills/
- *How to Write a Will: 7-Step Guide* https://www.nerdwallet.com/article/investing/estate-planning/how-to-write-a-will
- *Intestate Succession: Dying Without a Will* https://www.ramseysolutions.com/retirement/dying-without-a-will
- *5 potential benefits of a trust* https://www.usbank.com/wealth-management/financial-perspectives/trust-and-estate-planning/benefits-of-setting-up-a-trust.html

REFERENCES

- *Revocable Trust vs. Irrevocable Trust: What's the Difference?* https://www.investopedia.com/ask/answers/071615/what-difference-between-revocable-trust-and-living-trust.asp
- *How to Set Up a Trust: An Easy 8-Step Guide* https://copecorrales.com/articles/how-to-set-up-a-trust
- *Federal income tax and trust strategies | Trusts and taxes* https://www.fidelity.com/viewpoints/wealth-management/insights/trusts-and-taxes
- *Four Powerful Estate Planning Strategies for Single People* https://dworkenlaw.com/four-powerful-estate-planning-strategies-for-single-people/
- *Basic Estate Tax Planning For Married Couples* https://www.wardandsmith.com/articles/basic-estate-tax-planning-married-couples-use-estate-tax-exemptions
- *Estate Planning For Blended Families (Complete Guide)* https://www.trustworthy.com/blog/estate-planning-for-blended-families
- *Estate Planning for Unmarried Partners* https://www.estateplanning.com/estate-planning-for-unmarried-couples
- *Digital Asset: Meaning, Types, and Importance - Investopedia* https://www.investopedia.com/terms/d/digital-asset-framework.asp#:
- *Why You Must Put Digital Assets in Your Will or Estate Plan* https://www.aarp.org/home-family/personal-technology/info-2021/remember-digital-assets-in-your-will.html
- *How To Properly Manage Digital Assets* https://www.fastmetrics.com/blog/security/how-to-manage-digital-assets/
- *Estate planning for digital assets* https://www.fidelity.com/viewpoints/wealth-management/estate-planning-for-digital-assets
- *Estate Tax | Internal Revenue Service* https://www.irs.gov/businesses/small-businesses-self-employed/estate-tax
- *6 tips to help minimize estate taxes* https://www.fidelity.com/learning-center/personal-finance/how-to-avoid-estate-taxes
- *The essential guide to estate planning and income taxes* https://rsmus.com/insights/services/private-client/estate-planning-and-income-tax-key-considerations.html

- *Does Your State Have an Estate or Inheritance Tax?* https://taxfoundation.org/data/all/state/state-estate-tax-inheritance-tax-2022/
- *Types of Advance Directives* https://www.cancer.org/cancer/managing-cancer/making-treatment-decisions/advance-directives/types-of-advance-health-care-directives.html
- *If There is No Advance Directive or Guardian, Who Makes ...* https://www.americanbar.org/groups/law_aging/publications/bifocal/vol_37/issue_1_october2015/hospitalist_focus_group/
- *5 types of power of attorney, explained* https://www.freewill.com/learn/5-types-of-power-of-attorney
- *Advance Care Planning: Advance Directives for Health Care* https://www.nia.nih.gov/health/advance-care-planning/advance-care-planning-advance-directives-health-care
- *An Executor's Legal Duties | Probate Law Center* https://www.justia.com/probate/probate-administration/the-duties-of-an-executor-of-an-estate/
- *What is the difference between an estate executor and a ...* https://www.legalzoom.com/articles/what-is-the-difference-between-an-estate-executor-and-a-trustee
- *Should You Choose Family or a Professional Trustee ...* https://www.czepigalaw.com/blog/should-you-choose-family-or-a-professional-trustee-know-the-pros-and-cons/
- *Guidelines for Individual Executors & Trustees* https://www.americanbar.org/groups/real_property_trust_estate/resources/estate_planning/guidelines_for_individual_executors_trustees/
- *The Importance of Open Communication in Estate Planning* https://www.stoufferlegal.com/blog/the-importance-of-open-communication-in-estate-planning-balancing-transparency-and-discretion
- *Talking About Estate Planning - Tips from Fidelity* https://www.fidelity.com/life-events/estate-planning/talking-estate-planning
- *Five tips for talking to loved ones about estate planning* https://www.jsonline.com/story/news/solutions/2023/04/25/five-tips-for-talking-to-loved-ones-about-estate-planning/69791010007/

- *Estate Planning - How to Make a Family Meeting a Successful ...* https://wilsonlawgroup.com/make-family-meeting-successful-part-estate-planning-process/
- *7 Reasons It's Time To Update Your Estate Plan* https://www.forbes.com/sites/bobcarlson/2018/12/02/7-reasons-its-time-to-update-your-estate-plan/
- *6 life events that might impact your estate plan* https://www.edwardjones.com/us-en/market-news-insights/guidance-perspective/events-impacting-estate-plan
- *What is the best way to update my will?* https://www.nolo.com/legal-encyclopedia/what-the-best-update-will.html
- *Keep your health care directives up to date* https://www.health.harvard.edu/staying-healthy/keep-your-health-care-directives-up-to-date
- *Digital Asset Management in Life and Death* https://www.actec.org/resource-center/video/digital-asset-management-in-life-and-death/
- *Advantages and Disadvantages of Electronic Wills* https://petronilaw.com/advantages-and-disadvantages-of-electronic-wills/
- *How RUFADAA Is Changing Digital Estate Planning* https://www.kitces.com/blog/rufadaa-digital-estate-planning-rights-three-tiers-online-tool-fiduciary/
- *WealthCounsel Estate Planning Software, CLE and Legal ...* https://www.wealthcounsel.com/
- Nelson, Brett. 10 Inspirational Quotes About Estate Planning. Family Law, Divorce, Personal Injury in Texas. Last modified May 3, 2023. https://nelsonlawgrouppc.com/10-inspirational-quotes-about-estate-planning/.